Jesus: Crucified or Substituted?

Between Gnostic Thought and Islamic Theology

Jesus: Crucified or Substituted?

Between Gnostic Thought and Islamic Theology

E. R. Khalil

AGORA
UNIVERSITY
PRESS
EST. 2014

Jesus: Crucified or Substituted? Between Gnostic Thought and Islamic Theology

Copyright © 2021 by Agora University Press

All rights reserved. Printed in the United States of America. No part of this book may be used or reproduced in any manner whatsoever without written permission except in the case of brief quotations embodied in critical articles or reviews.

For information contact: aupress@agora.ac
Agora University Press: aupress.org

ISBN 978-1-950831-22-7

HIS HOLINESS POPE TAWADROS II
118th Pope and Patriarch of the great city of Alexandria and the See of St. Mark

HIS HOLINESS PATRIARCH IGNATIUS APHREM II
Patriarch of Antioch and All the East

v

Acknowledgments

A couple of years ago comparative religion sparked my interest, and most especially, Christian-Muslim dialogue as I live and work in a Muslim-majority country; I often engage in friendly discussions with Muslim colleagues and neighbors about the similarities and differences between Christianity and Islam. One of the most discussed topics among the differences between the two faiths is the crucifixion of Christ: was it real as Christians believe, or an illusion as Muslims believe? This question stuck in my head for some time. I kept wondering if there did exist a first-generation Christian group that believed in the illusion of the Crucifixion. I soon had the opportunity to investigate the matter in my master's thesis as part of my post-graduate studies in Orthodox Theology at Holy Transfiguration College, Agora University. Later, this study expanded to the book you now hold.

The only issue I faced during my course of study is that I found valuable resources related to the matter in Arabic without English translations. However, as my first language is Arabic, I could overcome this limitation.

This is a good chance to thank all of those who helped, supported, and encouraged me during writing my book. I would like to thank my advisor, Dr. Mary Ghattas, for her availability, valuable guidance, helpful advice, and support during this process. I also wish to thank all my family and friends who supported me and helped me until I finished my book.

I hope this study would be interesting and of good value to all those who are interested in comparative religion.

E. R. Khalil
November 8, 2020

Table of Contents

Acknowledgments..vii

Introduction...11

Replacing the Form, Escaping Crucifixion......22

Islam & Gnosticism..106

Conclusion..152

Bibliography..161

Introduction
Background

For Christians, the Crucifixion of Jesus Christ is not merely a historical event; rather, it bears a significant theological dimension. It is the event in which Christ defeated death as Vladimir Lossky writes: "on the cross, death is swallowed up in life. In Christ, death enters into divinity and there exhausts itself, for 'it does not find a place there.'"[1] Denying the Crucifixion is denying the defeat of death as it would still have the upper hand, but on the contrary, Christians do not fear death compared to those who do not believe in the Crucifixion and the Resurrection, to the extent

---

[1] Vladimir Lossky, *Orthodox Theology: An Introduction* (Crestwood: St. Vladimir's Seminary Press, 2002), 116.

that Paul writes: "to die is gain."[2] This can be examined when we look at the era of martyrdom during the first centuries of Christianity. Martyrs were certain that resurrection is the final step, not death, mirroring what happened with Jesus as Paul states: "for if we have been united with him in a death like his, we shall certainly be united with him in a resurrection like his."[3] The victory over death achieved after the Resurrection of Christ would never have happened without passing through death first.

Another significance of the Crucifixion is that sins were forgiven, because "indeed, under the law almost everything is purified with blood, and without the shedding of blood there is no forgiveness of sins."[4] Previously, forgiveness was achieved through the animal sacrifices of the Old Testament. The sacrificial death on the cross is the actualization of the symbolic ritual of the

---

[2] Phil. 1:21 ESV
[3] Rom. 6:5
[4] Heb. 9:22

Passover in the Old Testament as Lossky states: "Death on the cross is the Passover of the New Alliance, fulfilling in one reality all that is symbolized by the Hebrew Passover."[5] The Crucifixion gives meaning to what the animal sacrifices of the Old Testament were pointing at "for it is impossible for the blood of bulls and goats to take away sins."[6] So it was necessary for Jesus Christ as an innocent person to

> "assume all sin, 'substitutes' Himself for those who are justly condemned and suffers death for them. 'Behold the Lamb of God Who takes upon Himself the sins of the world,' says St. John the Baptist, echoing Isaiah."[7]

The entire sacrificial tradition of Israel culminates in the incident of the Crucifixion.[8]

Moreover, Christians consider certain Old Testament passages that speak of the suffering

---

[5] Lossky, Ibid.
[6] Heb. 10:4
[7] Lossky, Ibid., 110.
[8] Ibid.

and death of the Christ, as prophecies that were fulfilled in Jesus Christ. As an example, when Christ cried on the Cross "My God, my God, why hast Thou forsaken me?"[9] This cry can only be understood through the Old Testament text:

> "for the ultimate cry of the Crucified is none other than the first verse of Psalm 22, the prayer of the long-suffering man of righteousness. The beginning of this psalm proclaims human despair [...] Then follows the famous prophetic passage, the hands and feet pierced, the garments shared out, the tunic tossed for."[10]

For Christians, the Crucifixion does not only hold a theological significance but also relates to Old Testament prophetic passages which make the reality of the Crucifixion inevitable. In short, Lossky summarizes the importance of the Crucifixion for Christians by quoting St. Gregory of Nazianzen:

---

[9] Mark 15:34
[10] Lossky, Ibid., 112.

"This voluntary integration into the condition of fallen humanity had to end in the death on the cross, and the descent Into Hell. Thus, the whole of our fallen nature—death included—and all the existential consequences of sin, such as had the character of penalty, chastisement and curse, have been transformed by the cross of Christ into the means of our salvation. The cross which should stand for final decay, became the unshakable foundation of the universe: the life-giving cross, the power of Kings, the constancy of the righteous, the magnificence of priests."[11]

Research questions

The Crucifixion and the Resurrection of Christ are crucial events for the Christian faith. However, in early Christianity, certain beliefs appeared denying the reality of the incarnation and the Crucifixion of Christ claiming that these events were just an illusion. These beliefs came to

---

[11]Vladimir Lossky, *The Mystical Theology of the Eastern Church* (London: J Clarke, 2005), 154.

be known as Docetism, a basic doctrine in Gnosticism. Even though someone called Jesus Christ was historically crucified in reality under Pontius Pilate, Gnostics found it somehow problematic and difficult to grasp. They provided many explanations to justify their position despite the historical fact of the Crucifixion. One of the explanations is that Christ exchanged His form with another person who was crucified in His stead. So, it appeared to the people that Christ was crucified but He was not, this explanation is referred to as the Substitution Theory in this study. Irenaeus of Lyons, a second-century Church Father, mentioned such a claim in his work *Against Heresies* and attributed it to Basilides of Alexandria, a second-century Gnostic Christian leader.[12] On the other hand, Islam too

---

[12] Irenaeus of Lyons, *Against Heresies, Ante-Nicene Fathers: The Writings of the Fathers Down to A.D. 325,* Vol. 1. Eds. A.C. Coxe, J. Donaldson, A. Roberts, (Grand Rapids: Eerdmans Publishing, 1989), 349.

denies the Crucifixion of Christ stating in the Qu'ran:

> "that they said (in boast), 'We killed Christ Jesus the son of Mary, the Messenger of Allah;' but they killed him not, nor crucified him, but so it was made to appear to them... for of a surety they killed him not, nay, Allah raised him up unto Himself; and Allah is Exalted in Power, Wise."[13]

Since the dawn of Islam, this position forms a major difference between Christianity and Islam and ignites heated debates between the adherents of these two religions, but the debates on this topic did not emerge with Islam. Rather, the debates began in the second century of the current era when the idea of substitution first appeared among the Basilidians. It found popularity within Islam, where it exists today, after the gradual death of Gnosticism. Although there is a great deal of evidence that supports the historic reality of the Crucifixion of Christ,

---

[13] Qu'ran 4: 157, 158 - Yusuf Ali

Basilides rejected the idea of Christ being crucified claiming that someone else took Christ's form and was crucified in His stead, making the event nothing more than an illusion. I argue that Islam borrowed the Basilidian idea that was still popular in Arabia at the birth of Islam without considering neither the historicity of the Crucifixion, nor the theological background of such an illusionary doctrine.

Certain questions that must be raised in this debatable matter: what is the origin of such doctrine? Is there any historical link between Islam and Gnosticism with regards to Docetism? To what extent does this theory reflect the actual historical event according to the evidence and data that is available today? What are the arguments that support the Substitution Theory and their counterarguments? The answers to these questions should offer convincing evidence toward a certain position: either Jesus was crucified or not. So, we can narrow the purpose of this study to the answer to one question: to what extent does the Substitution Theory reflect what happened at the Crucifixion?

Methodology

The method used in this research to pursue the answers to its questions will be a combination of historical and systematic methods. We will examine different historical eras trying to find pieces of evidence that target the above-mentioned research questions. Since our main discussion will center on Gnostic and Islamic views of the Crucifixion, I will examine scholarly contributions on the topic. Gnostic and Islamic sacred texts and their interpretations of the Crucifixion will also be investigated. Also, the movement of certain Gnostic groups and ideas will be tracked historically to find a geographic connection between early Gnostic groups and the Arabian Peninsula. Systematically, certain theological concepts on the Substitution Theory in both Gnosticism and Islam will be considered as well as the background of this doctrine and its foundation. Also, the relation between both ideologies will be examined, especially through parallel ideas and stories.

Structure

As these matters must be presented in an organized manner to reach a definitive position regarding the Crucifixion of Christ, I managed to structure the book as follows: after this introductory chapter, chapter two, titled "Replacing the form, escaping the Crucifixion," mainly discusses the Substitution Theory and traces its origin. I will trace how Gnosticism derived the Substitution Theory from its Docetic doctrine. Afterward, I will delve into the founder of this theory. Then, I will shed some light on different Docetic views of the Crucifixion other than the Substitution Theory. Lastly, I will show how the earliest Orthodox Fathers responded to this theory.

The third and final chapter is titled "Islam and Gnosticism." Here I will scrutinize the relation between Gnosticism and Islam. First, a brief overview of Islamic theology will be presented, along with its basic principles, and its origin. Then, I will discuss the Islamic view on Jesus Christ and the Crucifixion. Afterward, I explore evidence on the existence of a relation between Gnosticism and Islam by discussing their theological parallels as well as the accessibility of Gnostic texts, thoughts, or groups by the Arabs around the birth of Islam. Then I will present suggestions on why Islam preferred the Substitution Theory over the Orthodox view.

Replacing the Form, Escaping the Crucifixion

History speaks

The traditional Orthodox view believed in the Crucifixion of Christ theologically and historically.[14] Gregory R. Lanier, referring to the Substitution Theory, states:

> "this dogma is not, however, without its difficulties: it requires rejection of the broad scholarly consensus that the Crucifixion of Jesus of Nazareth outside Jerusalem under the oversight of

---

[14] R. Van Den Broek, "The Present State of Gnostic Studies," *Vigiliae Christianae* 37, no. 1 (1983): 49. Orthodox view means the view of the apostles of Christ that was handed down from Christ to Christians through the ecclesiastical canonical fathers.

> Pontius Pilate is an indisputable historical fact."[15]

So, besides the theological dimension of the Crucifixion in Christian theology, it is almost unanimously a historical fact. N. T. Wright, in the first volume of his series *Christian Origins and the Question of God*, reconstructs the history of early Christianity and tracks its course. He puts fixed historical points from which he can move through the timeline and trace the movement and development of early Christianity. He asks: "where, then, are the fixed points around which we must work?"[16] He counts the Crucifixion as the initial and the most significant fixed historical point as he writes:

> "the Crucifixion sets not only the chronological and (in the full sense) historical starting-point for the

---

[15] Gregory R. Lanier, "'It Was Made to Appear Like That to Them:' Islam's Denial of Jesus' Crucifixion," *Reformed Faith & Practice*, accessed April 25, 2020, https://journal.rts.edu/article/it-was-made-to-appear-like-that-to-them-islams-denial-of-jesus-crucifixion-in-the-quran-and-dogmatic-tradition/.

[16] N. T. Wright, *The New Testament and the People of God*, (London: SPCK Publishing, 2013), 346.

movement: it also actually sets the tone for most of the major fixed points."[17]

From the very beginning of Christianity, the cross for the Orthodox Christians was one of the major symbols of Christianity. Justin Martyr, a second-century Church Fathers, writes in his first Apology: "this (the Cross) is the greatest symbol of His (Christ's) power and role; as is also proved by the things which fall under our observation."[18] Wright, commenting on Justin's quote states:

> "within a short time, the cross became the central Christian symbol, easy to draw, hard to forget, pregnant both in its reference to Jesus himself and in its multiple significance for his followers."[19]

---

[17] Ibid., 347.

[18] Justin Martyr, *The First Apology* 55, *Ante-Nicene Fathers: The Writings of the Fathers Down to A.D. 325*, Vol. 1. Eds. A.C. Coxe, J. Donaldson, A. Roberts, (Grand Rapids: Eerdmans Publishing, 1989), 181-182.

[19] Wright, Ibid., 367.

After long historical analysis about early Christianity, Wright assures that "the cross and resurrection, in short, are clearly central to virtually all known forms of early Christianity."[20]

Moreover, historical evidence regarding the Crucifixion is found in several ancient non-Christian documents of Greek, Roman, and Jewish sources. Although there are sources that speak of Jesus Christ as a historical figure generally, I will present only the sources specific to the Crucifixion. The first reference is by Thallos, a Greek historian who penned a three-volume chronicle around 55 AD ,mentioning the darkness that accompanied the Crucifixion of Christ as if it was just an eclipse of the sun.[21] Sextus Julius Africanus (160-240 AD), a Christian writer, advocated a different purpose of this darkness in response to Thallos' claim stating: "in the third

---

[20] Ibid., 400.
[21] Robert E. Van Voorst, *Jesus Outside the New Testament: An Introduction to the Ancient Evidence* (Grand Rapids: W.B. Eerdmans Publishing, 2000), 20. The canonical gospels mentioned that darkness that happened during the Crucifixion in Matthew 27:45, Mark 15:33, and Luke 23:44.

book of his histories, Thallos calls this darkness an eclipse of the sun, which seems to me to be wrong."[22] This darkness happened at the Passover which always falls at a full moon, and it is impossible to have a solar eclipse at a full moon, so Julius argues that the darkness, as mentioned in the canonical gospels, was a miracle of God.[23] Hence, the Crucifixion narratives according to the canonical gospels are correct and authentic, even detailing the natural phenomena around it, such as that miraculous darkness.

The second reference belongs to Cornelius Tacitus (56-120 AD), the greatest Roman historian, who has two partially surviving works, the *Histories* and the *Annals*.[24] In the *Annals*,

---

[22] Ibid. Most of Thallos' work was perished as well as the work of Julius Africanus, but these quotes reached us through the Chronicle (800 AD) of a Byzantine historian called Georgius Syncellus.

[23] Ibid., 20-21. Thallos could have mentioned the eclipse without referring to Jesus, but the context in Julius, as Robert E. Van Voorst concludes, shows that he is refuting Thallos' argument that the darkness is not religiously significant.

[24] Ibid., 39. The *Histories* records the reigns of a series of Roman Emperors between AD 69-96, while the *Annals* is an

Tacitus documents the burning of Rome that happened in the year 64 AD.[25] He states in chapter 44:

> "But neither human effort nor the emperor's generosity nor the placating of the gods ended the scandalous belief that the fire had been ordered. Therefore, to put down the rumor, Nero substituted as culprits and punished in the most unusual ways those hated for their shameful acts [*flagitia*], whom the crowd called "Chrestians."[26] The founder of this name, Christ, had been executed in the reign of Tiberius by the procurator Pontius Pilate [*Auctor nominis eius Christus Tiberio imperitante per procuratorem Pontium Pilatum supplicio adfectus erat*]."[27]

---

unfinished work treats the events between AD 14-68. Modern historians considers the *Annals* as the best source of information about this period.

[25] Ibid., 40, Tacitus mentions the burning of Rome in his book in chapters 38-45. Chapter 44 is the chapter where he mentions the Christians and Christ.

[26] "Chrestians" is written this way in the oldest manuscripts, not "Christians," see Van Voorst, Ibid., 44.

[27] Ibid., 41-42.

There was a rumor that Nero, the Roman Emperor, is the one who ordered the fire. Tacitus informs us that Nero turned the accusation to the Christians as they were generally regarded as a suspicious group in first century Rome.[28] He also mentions that "Christ had been executed in the reign of Tiberius by Pontius Pilate" which historically corroborates with the Crucifixion account in the canonical gospels. Tacitus in this passage speaks of Christ's execution as a well-known fact that he is informing the reader about. Although the authenticity of this passage has been disputed and some scholars claim that it was interpolated and edited at later times, the majority of scholars agree that it is accurate and trustworthy.[29]

The third historical testimony comes from a letter sent by a prisoner called Mara bar Serapion to his son who was also called

---

[28] Ibid., 41.
[29] Ibid., 42-43.

Serapion.[30] The letter was written in Syriac around 73 AD and its content indicates that the author was Stoic.[31] The part of the letter concerning the Crucifixion reads:

> "What advantage did the Athenians gain by murdering Socrates, for which they were repaid with famine and pestilence? Or the people of Samos by the burning of Pythagoras, because their country was completely covered in sand in just one hour? Or the Jews [by killing][32] their wise king, because their kingdom was taken away at that very time? God justly repaid the wisdom of these three men: the Athenians died of famine; the Samians were completely overwhelmed by the sea; and the Jews, desolate and driven from their own kingdom, are scattered through every nation. Socrates is not dead, because of Plato; neither is Pythagoras, because of the statue of Juno; nor is the wise king,

---

[30] Ibid., 53.
[31] Ibid. The only surviving manuscript is dates to the seventh century CE and is housed in the British Museum.
[32] Ibid., 54. Van Voorst states that "the Syriac lacks a verb in this clause, but the strong parallel with how Socrates and Pythagoras died makes it plain that killing is meant here."

because of the new laws he laid down."³³

The author here finds similarities between Jesus, Socrates, and Pythagoras; each of them was rejected and killed by his people and as a consequence, his people suffered justly by God. Although Jesus is not mentioned by name in Mara's letter, it can be understood that the above-mentioned "wise king" of the Jews refers to Jesus.³⁴ Also, the connection between the Jews' rejection of Jesus and the destruction of their kingdom is a Christian view that was mentioned implicitly in the Gospels and explicitly by Justin Martyr as well as later Church writers.³⁵

---

³³ Ibid.
³⁴ In the Gospels, Jesus often referred to as a king of the Jews, Israel, or Jerusalem, as one of His titles. The wise men called Him king of the Jews (Matthew 2:2), in His trial, Pilate asked Him if He was the king of the Jews (Matthew 27:11), the Roman soldiers were mocking Him saying "Hail, King of the Jews!" (Matthew 27:29), on the cross they placed a written charge over His head that read: "This is Jesus, the King of the Jews." (Matthew 27:37), and in many other places such as Matthew 27:42; Mark 15:9; Mark 15:12; John 12:15; John 19:14,15. However, this title was the least used by His disciples or by Himself.
³⁵ Van Voorst, Ibid., 55.

Moreover, speaking of the new laws most probably means the Christian moral teachings that Jesus taught.[36] Thus, it can be concluded from the letter of bar Serapion that the story of the Jews killing Jesus was a well-known and widespread fact.

The fourth testimony comes from a book called *The Death of Peregrinus* written by a well-known Greek satirist called Lucian of Samosata (115-200 AD).[37] Peregrinus was a popular figure who embraced Christianity then left it for Cynicism and political revolution.[38] Lucian writes for following about Peregrinus:

> "He (Peregrinus) was second only to that one whom they still worship today, the man in Palestine who was crucified because he brought this new form of initiation into the world."[39]

---

[36] Ibid.
[37] Ibid., 58, Lucian was a satirist and a traveling lecturer. He had more than eighty works, most of them are genuinely belonged to him. He used to criticize the faults and weaknesses of his time.
[38] Ibid.
[39] Ibid., 59.

Lucian here describes how Peregrinus became an important religious man in the Church to the extent that he became second to Jesus. He also refers to Jesus as the man who was crucified. In another part of the book, he mentions what Christ taught the Christians:

> "the first lawgiver of theirs persuaded them that they are all brothers the moment they transgress and deny the Greek gods and begin worshipping that crucified sophist and living by his laws."[40]

Although using the title "Sophist" is part of his satire, Lucian mentions the Crucifixion again as a major characteristic or part of Christ's identity calling Him the "crucified Sophist."

The fifth historical witness comes from the Jewish historian Josephus (37-100 AD).[41] The two

---

[40] Ibid.
[41] Ibid., 81. Josephus' original name was Joseph ben Mattathias, he belonged to a priestly family, he was a leader in the Jewish revolt against Rome, but later he took the opposite direction and embraced the Roman cause, became

chief works of Josephus are *The Jewish War* and *Antiquities of the Jews*. The latter bears witness to Christ in two passages, one passage mentions Jesus briefly as a brother of James while the other passage speaks about Him more extensively.[42] The extensive passage, known as "Witness of Flavius (Josephus)" [*Testimonium Flavianum*], is found in his work *Antiquities* Book 18, Chapter 3.[43] This specific passage is very problematic and has always been disputed as it is difficult to confirm its authenticity due to the lack of its old manuscripts.[44] Besides, after the rising of historical criticism in modern times, scholars started to view this passage as interpolated by Christians, a view that gradually gained popularity and earned wide support until it became dominant among scholars.[45] That is why there are many versions of this passage as many

---

a Roman citizen and held a position closer to the emperor as a writer, and his name became Flavius Josephus.
[42] Ibid., 82, 83.
[43] Ibid., 84.
[44] Ibid., 88.
[45] Ibid., 89.

scholars tried to reconstruct the original writing of Josephus without the Christian interpolations.⁴⁶ The standard and most popular version reads as follows:

> "Now there was about this time Jesus, a wise man, if it be lawful to call him a man; for he was a doer of wonderful works, a teacher of such men as receive the truth with pleasure. He drew over to him both many of the Jews and many of the Gentiles. He was [the] Christ. And when Pilate, at the suggestion of the principal men amongst us, had condemned him to the cross, those that loved him at the first did not forsake him; for he appeared to them alive again the third day; as the divine prophets had foretold these and ten thousand other wonderful things concerning him. And the tribe of Christians, so named from him, are not extinct at this day."⁴⁷

---

⁴⁶ Ibid., 84-101. In these pages, Van Voorst presented different forms of the suggested reconstructed passages of Testimonium Flavianum and critically analyzed them.

⁴⁷ Flavius Josephus, *Antiquities of the Jews* 18.3.3, trans. William Whiston, *The Complete Works of Josephus* (Grand Rapids: Kregel Publications, 1981), 379.

The scope of this study is concerned with this statement: "and when Pilate [...] had condemned him to the cross." This statement mentioning Crucifixion remains constant throughout the different attempts to reconstruct the original passage by Josephus.[48] What that means is that the part relating to the Crucifixion of Christ most probably is an authentic statement of Josephus, written as a well-known fact by a contemporary historian.

The sixth and last witness that will be discussed in this section comes from Talmudic literature. The Talmud is a collection of rabbinic literature that was compiled in stages.[49] The first stage falls between the first century BC until about 200 AD and it is called the "Tannaitic" period in which the Jewish oral traditions and the

---

[48] Van Voorst, Ibid., 84–101.
[49] Ibid., 106.

Mishna was compiled.[50] However, some Tannaitic teachings of this period were not recorded in its stage. These teachings were rather recorded in the stage following the Tannaitic period, known as the Amoraic period, in which the Mishna commentaries, the Gemara, was compiled.[51] The Gemara contains commentaries on the Mishna and Tannaitic traditions. Among those traditions

---

[50] "Tanna | Judaic Scholar," *Encyclopedia Britannica*, accessed September 11, 2020, https://www.britannica.com/topic/tanna-Judaic-scholar, "Tannaitic" comes from the Aramaic word "Tanna" which means "teacher" refering to the Jewish scholars who compiled the Mishna. The "Mishna" is part of the Talmud which is the Jewish oral traditions and laws that was preserved orally for centuries before written down as the Mishna.

[51] Van Voorst, Ibid., 107; "Amora | Jewish Scholar," *Encyclopedia Britannica*, accessed September 12, 2020, https://www.britannica.com/topic/amora, "Amoraic" comes from the Aramaic word "Amora" which means "interpreter" or "reciter" refering to the Jewish scholars who compiled the Gemara which is interpretations of and commentaries on the Mishna. There are two Gemaras, one was compiled in Jerusalem and the other one in Babylon, when integrated with the Mishna formed two Talmuds, the Jerusalem Talmud (Talmud Yerushalmi) and the Babylonian Talmud respectively.

is a passage concerning the Crucifixion of Christ exists in the Babylonian Talmud:

> "It was taught: On the day before the Passover they hanged Jesus. A herald went before him for forty days [proclaiming], 'He will be stoned, because he practiced magic and enticed Israel to go astray. Let anyone who knows anything in his favor come forward and plead for him.' But nothing was found in his favor, and they hanged him on the day before the Passover" (b. Sanhédrin 43a).[52]

The previous passage portrays the trial of Jesus differently than in the canonical gospels. Here, the trial was publicly announced forty days before it took place whereas in the canonical gospels, the trial was carried out secretly and suddenly.[53] Van Voorst reads this story of the trial as "an apologetic response to Christian statements about an unjust trial."[54] He also points

---

[52] Van Voorst, Ibid., 114.
[53] Matthew 26; Mark 14; Luke 22; John 18.
[54] Van Voorst, Ibid., 118.

out that this passage is referring to the Crucifixion by stating that "the passage refers at its beginning and end to 'hanging,' a Hebrew-Aramaic approximation of crucifixion."[55]

Finally, after presenting these six ancient non-Christian attestations that support the historical reality of the Crucifixion, varying between Roman, Greek, and Jewish perspectives, we can confidently say that the Crucifixion of Christ is an irrefutable historical fact despite the variations of the details around the event. On the other hand, the Substitution Theory came into the scene at some point in time denying that Jesus was truly crucified and that someone else was crucified in His stead. It is important now to trace this idea to investigate the authenticity of its source.

---

[55] Ibid., 119.

Origin of the Theory

Searching in history for the origin of a specific theory or certain idea is no easy task, most especially when we do not have enough resources for the probable date of origin of this idea, as is the case in early Christianity. Wright acknowledges that far less is known about the history of the church from 30-135 AD than is known about second-temple Judaism and the sources we do have are scarce in comparison with the Jewish material.[56] Despite this, the information that we seek can be extracted from the sources at hand today. The Substitution Theory was found among the writings of Irenaeus of Lyons. He writes the following passage regarding a certain belief attributing it to someone called Basilides:

> "Basilides again, that he may appear to have discovered something more sublime and plausible, gives an immense development to his doctrines. He

---

[56] Wright, Ibid., 341.

> sets forth that Nous was the firstborn of the unborn father [...] Wherefore he (Christ) did not himself suffer death, but Simon, a certain man of Cyrene, being compelled, bore the cross in his stead; so that this latter being transfigured by him, that he might be thought to be Jesus, was crucified, through ignorance and error, while Jesus himself received the form of Simon, and, standing by, laughed at them. For since he was an incorporeal power, and the Nous (mind) of the unborn father, he transfigured himself as he pleased, and thus ascended to him who had sent him."[57]

According to the previous passage, Basilides states that Jesus exchanged His form with Simon of Cyrene who bore the cross and was crucified instead of Jesus, whereas Jesus escaped crucifixion and ascended to the Father. Who is Basilides and how did he develop this thought?

---

[57] Irenaeus of Lyons, *Against Heresies* 1.24.4 , *Ante-Nicene Fathers: The Writings of the Fathers Down to A.D. 325, Vol. 1.* Eds. A.C. Coxe, J. Donaldson, A. Roberts, (Grand Rapids: Eerdmans Publishing, 1989), 349.

The following sections will attempt to answer this question, after first introducing Gnosticism and the collection of beliefs that affected Basilides' thought.

Who are the Gnostics?

Defining Gnosticism today is not as simple as it was decades ago. Edwin M Yamauchi acknowledges that on the one hand, there are those who would define Gnosticism very narrowly and, on the other hand, there are those who would define the phenomenon quite broadly. Thus, one man's Gnosticism may be simply another man's Mysticism, Esoterism, Docetism, or Encratism.[58] Scholars who adopt the narrow definition of Gnosticism will reject the existence of pre-Christian Gnosticism while those who tend to define Gnosticism broadly will find its traces

---

[58] Edwin M Yamauchi, *Pre-Christian Gnosticism: A Survey of the Proposed Evidences* (Eugene: Wipf & Stock Publishers, 2003), 13.

before Christianity as well as in many early texts including the New Testament.[59]

Gnosticism today cannot simply be defined as a Christian heresy due to the current academic discussion. This difficulty in defining Gnosticism does not predate the Twentieth century as Gnosticism was presented in the writings of the Church Fathers as a Christian heresy.[60] Among scholars, there was almost a consensus that it was a Christian heresy, at least before 1966. That same year, the International Conference on the Origins of Gnosticism met in Messina, Italy, in an attempt to define and standardize the use of two terms, pre-Gnostic and proto-Gnostic, among scholars. Yet not all scholars accepted such terms and their definitions.[61] The conference defined the term pre-Gnostic as elements of pre-Christian beliefs that later were incorporated into Gnostic

---

[59] Ibid., 13, 14.
[60] Ibid., 20.
[61] Ibid., 18.

developed systems, whereas proto-Gnostic was defined as primitive forms of Gnosticism existed before the fully developed systems of the second century.[62] In 1978, the International Conference on Gnosticism was held at Yale University to "rediscover Gnosticism."[63] Among the presenters at this conference was one Helmut Koester, who examined sayings of Jesus in Gnostic sources and argued that not all sayings that lack parallels in the canonical gospels are to be considered late and heretical.[64] His idea that gave the impression of overlapping traditions between Orthodox Christianity and Gnosticism.

Although there is no clear-cut unanimous definition of Gnosticism among scholars, it can generally be described as a syncretistic collection of thought that took unto itself many elements from many sources and assumed many forms. It

---

[62] Ibid.
[63] "Colloquia: The International Conference on Gnosticism at Yale: A Report," *The Biblical Archaeologist* 42, no. 4 (1979): 253.
[64] Ibid., 254.

is, therefore, impossible to speak of a single type of Gnosticism.⁶⁵ That is why we can find Gnostic groups appeared in certain phases in many religions like Paganism, Judaism, and Christianity, but it was in Christianity that it grew most aggressive.⁶⁶ Gnostic thought certainly existed before Christianity, but no evidence shows the existence of such thoughts combined into a coherent system as compared to those of the second century AD.⁶⁷

Gnostic Christianity is developed out of Hellenistic syncretism.⁶⁸ Almost all the Gnostic Christian converts came from a pagan worldview, they were all Gentiles, not Jews, without exception, and their prominent founders were

---

⁶⁵ Williston Walker et al., *A History of the Christian Church* (New York: Scribner, 1959), 54.
⁶⁶ Samuel Angus, *The Religious Quests of the Graeco-Roman World: A Study in the Historical Background of Early Christianity.* (New York: Biblo and Tannen, 1967), 377.
⁶⁷ R. McL Wilson, "Gnostic Origins Again," *Vigiliae Christianae* 11, no. 2 (1957): 96.
⁶⁸ Ibid., 97.

natives of Syria or Egypt.⁶⁹ The sects of the Gnostic Christianity of the second century AD were also not one defined system, but they were numerous and each sect varied in some aspects from the other, but they all have some fundamental features.⁷⁰ There existed more than fifty distinct Gnostic sects of which the Basilidians, the Valentinians, the Marcionites, and the Manicheans, are the most prominent.⁷¹

One of the most important basic features among Gnostic sects is that salvation is achieved through secret knowledge, which Christ imparted to His disciples orally, as Gaye Strathearn attests:

> "a number of Gnostic texts, including the Gospel of Judas, indicate that salvation comes, not from Jesus' Atonement and Resurrection, but from a secret

---

[69] Edward Gibbon and J. B. Bury, *The History of the Decline and Fall of the Roman Empire*, vol. 2, (London : Methuen & Co. , 1901), 13,
//catalog.hathitrust.org/Record/009793910.
[70] Wilson, "Gnostic Origins Again," 100.
[71] Gibbon and Bury, Ibid., 14. The Manichean sect appeared at a later time.

knowledge that Jesus imparted to a selected group of his followers."[72]

It is not mere knowledge but,

"mystical, supernatural wisdom, by which the initiates were brought to a true understanding of the universe and were saved from this evil world of matter [...] be freed from this bondage to the visible world[...] into communion with the true realm of spiritual realities."[73]

From this definition of mystical knowledge comes the term Gnosis [Greek: γνῶσις] which literally means "knowledge," the term that refers to the whole ideology of Gnosticism.[74] However, it is difficult to trace back the origin of such an idea, as Samuel Angus acknowledges that scholarship has devoted much attention to the question of the origin of Gnosticism, but, generally speaking, with

---

[72] Gaye Strathearn, "The Gnostic Context of the Gospel of Judas," *Brigham Young University Studies* 45, no. 2 (2006): 28.
[73] Walker et al., Ibid., 54.
[74] Ibid.

unsatisfactory results.[75] Since we are here concerned with Gnostic Christianity specifically, and not Gnosticism in general, we will focus on the beginning of Gnostic Christianity; from now on, the term Gnosticism will signify Gnostic Christianity for our purposes.

Williston Walker suggests that the initial spark of Gnosticism (Gnostic Christianity) is an attempt to solve the issue of the apparent confusion between the earthly humiliating life of Jesus and the pre-existent glorified Christ,[76] they simply denied the reality of His earthly life. They admitted that Christ came to Earth, lived among us, and taught His disciples, but as a heavenly being and not with our human nature.[77]

Another probability is that Gnosticism was a product of misinterpretations of the apostolic writings. One of the prime apostolic texts that

---

[75] Angus, Ibid., 379.
[76] Walker et al., Ibid., 53.
[77] Ibid.

sounds like Gnosticism is that of the first epistle of Paul to the Corinthians:

> "However, we speak wisdom among those who are mature, yet not the wisdom of this age, nor of the rulers of this age, who are coming to nothing. But we speak the wisdom of God in a mystery, the hidden wisdom which God ordained before the ages for our glory, which none of the rulers of this age knew; for had they known, they would not have crucified the Lord of glory."[78]

In the previous passage, Masud Masihiyyen states that Paul actually meant to correlate the hidden wisdom and its revelation with the salvation of Christ by the means of His Crucifixion,

> "but Gnostics twisted Paul's theological implications to reach the conclusion that salvation in Christ was only through the revelation of some secret teachings [...] Paul's remarks neither denied the Crucifixion nor changed the

---
[78] 1 Cor. 2:6-10

mystery of salvation into the means of salvation."⁷⁹

In the same vein, Rudolf Karl Bultmann agrees that Gnosticism was produced within the Church, which leads to a similar conclusion that it was a product of textual misinterpretation:

> "Gnosticism is combatted not as if it were a foreign, heathen religion into which Christians are in danger of apostatizing. Rather, it is only dealt with so far as it is a phenomenon within Christianity."⁸⁰

Another proposed suggestion comes from early Christian writers who denounced Simon Magus as the father of all heresies.⁸¹ However, scholars find difficulties in relating the mythological system attributed to Simon in the

---

[79] Masud Masihiyyen, "Immature Resurrection of Gnosticism in Islam," sec. 2, accessed May 11, 2020, https://www.answering-islam.org/authors/masihiyyen/gnostic_islamic_crucifixion.html. Masud is a former Muslim who embraced Christianity and wrote many comparative religion articles.
[80] Wilson, Ibid., 95.
[81] Ibid., 107.

early Christian writings—in which he stands as a divine redeemer—to the historical Simon presented in Acts as simply and purely a magician.[82] Some theories propose either there was a development in his system or the opposite, he was not promoted from magician to divine redeemer, but degraded in the Christian tradition from divine redeemer to plain magician.[83]

In seeking the process of development of the Gnostic Christianity, Robert McLachlan Wilson notices the first distant clash in I Corinthians, and then a prime form of Gnosticism is attacked in the later books of the New Testament, with the storm reaching its peak in the second century.[84] Although second-century Gnosticism had its strongest presence, it was divided into many groups and branches with differences and commonalities.

---

[82] Ibid., 108.
[83] Ibid.
[84] Ibid., 97. Robert McLachlan Wilson was Professor of New Testament, and then Professor of Biblical Criticism in the university St. Andrews and has many publications.

Basic Principles of Gnosticism

Tuomas Rasimus sums up the main components of Gnosticism despite its multiple branches of thought.[85] He states that they believe in a dualistic worldview, there are good that fights evil. They view the materialistic world—the human body included—as evil, in contrast with the spiritual world. They behave in extremely opposing ethics, either a rigorous ascetic way of life or an extreme libertine lifestyle. Their chief view about the creation is that of the Demiurge, an evil creator who is ranked below the true God.[86] However, some milder Gnostics such as Basilides view the Creator as an ignorant being who was unaware and unconscious of the true God, but he was not evil, yet he was somehow controlled by the true God unconsciously to execute His plan.[87] Gnostics also believe that

---

[85] April D De Conick, *Religion: Secret Religion*, 2016, 56, http://link.galegroup.com/apps/pub/8NWM/GVRL?sid=gale_marc&u=crepuq_mcgill.
[86] Ibid.
[87] Abraham P. Bos, "Basilides as an Aristotelianizing Gnostic," *Vigiliae Christianae* 54, no. 1 (2000): 56; Augustus

there are divine sparks in the materialistic world that need wake-up calls.[88] The good God is the head of the spiritual realm, the "Pleroma".[89] Early Gnosticism divided humankind into two divisions; "spiritual" who can be saved, and "material" who can never be saved, Later schools of Gnosticism like the one of Valentinus, added a third intermediate type who is "capable of faith, and of a certain degree of salvation."[90] Gnostics have also their own sacred texts but it is considered non-canonical by the Orthodox Church.

Non-canonical Christian texts

The non-canonical Christian literature is known as the Christian apocryphal texts. Apocrypha is a Greek word that means hidden things or secrets. Initially, it was used to denote

---

Neander and Henry John Rose, *The History of the Christian Religion and Church during the First Three Centuries* (London: St. Paul's Church-yard, 1841), 60.
[88] De Conick, Ibid., 56.
[89] Walker et al., Ibid., 55.
[90] Ibid.

esoteric books that should not be disclosed to the public, but only to the sect from which these books were initiated.[91] Usually, when these books became public, they appeared under the name of the apostles of Jesus to gain credibility and acceptance. However, when it became known that these books were falsely attributed to the apostles, the word apocrypha became an indication of the falsehood of the attribution and the unreliability of the content. Along with this indication of the term, the Church Fathers used it to indicate other meanings like writings containing useful facts along with doctrinal errors, writings not allowed to be publicly read in church, since not canonical, and writings that were heretical or used by heretics.[92] Many of these apocryphal texts were either pious imagination to the lacking details of the life of Christ or Mary and Joseph or the missionary

---

[91] Fr. Tadros Y. Malaty, *A Panoramic View Of Patristics In The First Six Centuries*, (Alexandria: St. George's Coptic Church Sporting, 2005), 21.
[92] Ibid.

journeys of the apostles that were not fulfilled by the canonical Scriptures, or gospels, acts, and visions written by various heretics of different schools of thoughts to support their position.[93] Based on the previous definition, the Gnostic texts are considered apocryphal by the Orthodox Church.

In 1945, the Nag Hammadi corpus, containing Gnostic texts was discovered in Nag Hammadi, Egypt. Prior to this discovery, all of our knowledge about Gnosticism used to come only from the Orthodox Fathers who defended Christianity against different Gnostic sects.[94] However, after the discovery, things started to change as Rasimus writes:

> "the discovery of thirteen papyrus codices near Nag Hammadi, Egypt, in 1945 and their publication in the 1960s and 1970s began to change things. The codices were soon identified as mainly gnostic, and suddenly scholars had ready access

---
[93] Ibid., 22.
[94] Strathearn, Ibid., 28.

to the ancient Gnostics' own voices."[95]

These texts also present a significantly different view than that of the canonical tradition. As an example, the serpent in the story of the Garden of Eden was portrayed as a good entity because it encourages Eve to gain knowledge by eating from the tree of knowledge of good and evil.[96] Consequently, it is evil and has a bad reputation in the canonical texts. The same paradox can be found in the Coptic Gospel of Judas that was discovered in the late 1970s in Egypt which historians believe that it goes back to the second century.[97] It portrays Judas as a hero for betraying Jesus and the other twelve disciples are inferior to him.[98]

In the same manner, the story of the Crucifixion according to the canonical gospels is

---

[95] De Conick, Ibid., 56.
[96] Strathearn, Ibid., 29.
[97] David Frankfurter, "An Historian's View of the 'Gospel of Judas,'" *Near Eastern Archaeology* 70, no. 3 (2007): 174.
[98] Strathearn, Ibid., 29.

different than that portrayed in the apocryphal gospel accounts. Although the passion narratives in the three synoptic gospels are slightly different in some minor details than that in John, the fourth Gospel, they all agree on the basic details. Eric D. Huntsman states that

> "while all four Gospels agree on the work of Jesus —namely that He died for the sins of the world and conquered death through the Resurrection— they focus on different aspects of His role as the Son of God."[99]

Huntsman mentions the distinctive features of the Gospel of John that make it unique from the other synoptic Gospels, one of these features that is related to the suffering and the sacrificial death of Christ is the thematic symbolism of Jesus as the Lamb of God:

> "Jesus is explicitly identified as the Lamb of God at the beginning of the Gospel, and this symbolism

---

[99] Eric D. Huntsman, ""The Lamb of God: Unique Aspects of the Passion Narrative in John," in Behold the Lamb of God: An Easter Celebration," 49–70, accessed October 18, 2020, https://rsc.byu.edu/behold-lamb-god/lamb-god-unique-aspects-passion-narrative-john#_edn41.

reemerges implicitly at the end of the Gospel, where the focus is on Jesus's sacrificial death, where Jesus, like a Paschal Lamb, sheds His blood so that death—spiritual as well as physical—may pass over His people."[100]

So as the canonical gospels are clear about the passion and death of Christ, most of the non-canonical Gnostic texts deny these happenings, confirming the escape of Christ from the Crucifixion either by interpreting the event docetically or by acknowledging a temporary dwelling of Christ in Jesus and His ascent just before the Crucifixion.

For instance, the *Apocalypse of Peter* contains a Docetic interpretation of the Crucifixion. We are here concerned with the Coptic *Apocalypse of Peter* that was found among Nag Hammadi Library, not to be confused with the Ethiopic early second-century text that bears

---

[100] Ibid.

the same name, as they are two different texts.[101] The date of origin of the Coptic Apocalypse of Peter is not certain, some scholars date it back to the third century, while others to the second century.[102]

In the *Second Treatise of the Great Seth* *(Sec. Seth)*, the story of the Crucifixion is similar to that attributed to Basilides.[103] That is why it is considered to be a Basilidian text but written in a later period than *Against Heresies*, which is the closing of the second century or early third century.[104] However, the treatise contains elements from the Valentinian tradition and other contradicting thoughts that make it difficult to be exclusively categorized under a certain Gnostic

---

[101] David Fiensy, "Lex Talionis in the 'Apocalypse of Peter,'" *The Harvard Theological Review* 76, no. 2 (1983): 255.
[102] Henriette W Havelaar, *The Coptic Apocalypse of Peter: Nag-Hammadi-Codex VII (3)*, 2012, 16, https://doi.org/10.1515/9783110884449.
[103] De Conick, Ibid., 65.
[104] Frederik Wisse, "The Nag Hammadi Library and the Heresiologists," *Vigiliae Christianae* 25, no. 3 (1971): 209, 218.

group.[105] A common theme found in the Gnostic texts like *Gospel of Judas, Apocalypse of Peter*, and *Sec. Seth* is that they all reject the Creator, considering him as a lesser god inferior to the ultimate God.[106]

It is important to also bring the Gospel of Barnabas into examination as we discuss the non-canonical gospels. Although this gospel was written as late as the sixteenth century and found in Italian and Spanish, it gained popularity and support by Muslim apologists as it strongly supports Islamic beliefs and views.[107] This gospel referred to Judas Iscariot as the one who was crucified instead of Jesus.[108] Many Muslim apologists argue that this gospel is authentic since it goes in line with Islamic theology, but the evidence proves otherwise. The story of the

---

[105] Ibid., 220.
[106] Frank Williams, "The Gospel of Judas: Its Polemic, Its Exegesis, and Its Place in Church History," *Vigiliae Christianae* 62, no. 4 (2008): 396.
[107] K. Prosser, *Was Jesus Crucified?* (Lulu.com, 2016), 153, https://books.google.com.eg/books?id=KsGyDAAAQBAJ.
[108] Ibid., 154.

Crucifixion presented in this gospel is not supported by the canonical gospels, nor the Gnostic texts, nor the vast majority of the Muslim commentators.[109] However, in the Gospel of Barnabas along with the previously mentioned apocryphal gospels, the common view of the Crucifixion is Docetic.

Docetic Views

Docetism is a common feature among all the Gnostic groups.[110] Docetism is a concept that started by the end of the first century.[111] The term comes from the Greek word *dokein* [Greek: δοκεῖν] which literally means "to seem."[112] Walker describes Docetism as certain views that "denied His (Jesus) real humanity and His actual death. He had not come 'in the flesh,' but in ghost-

---

[109] Ibid., 156.
[110] Malaty, Ibid., 185.
[111] S. Kent Brown and C. Wilfred Griggs, "The Apocalypse of Peter: Introduction and Translation," *Brigham Young University Studies* 15, no. 2 (1975): 136.
[112] "Docetism | Religion | Britannica," accessed July 1, 2020, https://www.britannica.com/topic/Docetism.

like, Docetic appearance."[113] He was only a spirit who appeared—seemed—to have a body of flesh, although various forms of this heresy existed.[114] The first epistle of John seems to refute the Docetic claims:

> "Beloved, do not believe every spirit, but test the spirits to see whether they are from God, for many false prophets have gone out into the world. By this, you know the Spirit of God: every spirit that confesses that Jesus Christ has come in the flesh is from God."[115]

This passage promotes the reality of the flesh of Christ against the illusionary form of Docetism.

Ignatius of Antioch writes in his Epistle to the Trallians "who was truly born and ate and drank. He was truly persecuted under Pontius Pilate; He was truly crucified."[116] The repetition

---

[113] Walker et al., Ibid., 53.
[114] Brown and Griggs, "The Apocalypse of Peter: Introduction and Translation," 136.
[115] 1 John 4: 2-3
[116] Ignatius of Antioch, *Epistle to the Trallians* 9 Ante-Nicene Fathers: The Writings of the Fathers Down to A.D. 325, Vol. 1.

of the word "truly" seems to confirm the reality of these events against the illusionary interpretations of the Docetic views. Ignatius has asked his followers to flee from those who say "that He (Jesus) only seemed to suffer."[117] He explicitly refers to the Docetic beliefs "as certain unbelievers maintain, that He only seemed to suffer, as they themselves only seem to be [Christians]."[118] The descriptor "certain unbelievers" may signify that they were already separated from the Orthodox community of believers, the Church, as a result of a schism as Wright concludes that Ignatius saw the Church:

> "suffering from potential and actual schism, caused partly by those who were mixing Christianity up with Judaism and partly by those who were preaching Docetism, the idea that Jesus had

---

Eds. A.C. Coxe, J. Donaldson, A. Roberts, (Grand Rapids: Eerdmans Publishing, 1989), 69-70.

[117] Ibid., chaps. 10, 11.
[118] Ignatius of Antioch, *Epistle to the Smyrnaeans* 2 *Ante-Nicene Fathers: The Writings of the Fathers Down to A.D. 325, Vol. 1.* Eds. A.C. Coxe, J. Donaldson, A. Roberts, (Grand Rapids: Eerdmans Publishing, 1989), 87.

only seemed to be, without really being, truly human."[119]

However, this view is not without a basis, as Gnosticism has certain fundamental doctrines that lead to such a Docetic view of Christ.

Identity of the Gnostic Jesus Christ

Generally, Gnosticism views Christ as the firstborn of God (whether they call Him Logos or Nous), the highest spiritual being in the Pleroma second to God, who extends himself through a succession of subordinate powers.[120] Cerinthus describes Christ as "the Logos or Spirit of God" as one identity.[121] And since the materialistic world is evil and Christ belongs to the good divine realm, so there is no way for him to be directly incarnated into the physical world. This belief

---

[119] Wright, Ibid., 351.
[120] Henry Longueville Mansel, *The Gnostic Heresies of the First and Second Centuries*, ed. J. B Lightfoot (London: John Murray, 1875), 18.
[121] Neander and Rose, Ibid., 52. It seems that was a common term among many Jewish theologians as written in the footnotes.

resulted in different views intended to explain how He appeared on Earth. The main Docetic views of Christ are as Walker puts them:

> "His appearance either as Docetic and ghostly, or as a temporary indwelling of the man Jesus, or as an apparent birth from a virgin mother without partaking of material nature."[122]

Gnostic Christians generally thought that Christ's mission was very specific—He came to bring "the true knowledge," so that "by his teaching, those capable of receiving it are restored to the Pleroma."[123]

Carpocrates, Cerinthus, and the Ebionites believed in Christ's indwelling the man Jesus. This belief states that the divine Christ descended from heaven and united Himself with the man Jesus at the time of his baptism.[124] Carpocrates' also taught that Jesus was a mere man, the son of Joseph and Mary, and that he was able to escape

---

[122] Walker et al., Ibid., 55.
[123] Ibid.
[124] Brown and Griggs, Ibid., 136.

the evil creator angels by virtue of a divine power that had descended into him,[125] whereas the Docetic view of Jesus, as discussed before, considers Him as "only a spirit who appeared—seemed—to have a body of flesh."[126] This view was adopted by Satornilus who taught that the Savior was unborn, incorporeal and without figure, and that it was in appearance only that He was seen as a man.[127] These Docetic views on Christ reject His humanity and consequently extend to His Crucifixion, the ultimate testimony of His Incarnation; how else could He be crucified without a body?

Docetic Views on the Crucifixion

The traditional Orthodox view recognizes the Crucifixion as historical reality in which Jesus Christ himself, not another, was crucified, truly

---

[125] De Conick, Ibid., 65.
[126] Brown and Griggs, Ibid.
[127] Glanville Downey, *A History of Antioch in Syria: From Seleucus to the Arab Conquest.*, xvii, 752 p. (Princeton: Princeton University Press, 1961), 291.

and physically suffered until He died, and He rose again from death. The Docetic narrative has a variety of views, some of which are a later development in explaining the Crucifixion event. The earliest Docetic view believed that Christ only "seems" to have a body because ultimately, He is a spiritual being. Therefore, He also "seems" to suffer in appearance only, not in reality. Docetae did not deny the Crucifixion of Christ but depicted it as a non-physical activity in which Christ pretended to be suffering. This view was refuted by the earliest apologetic writings against Docetism of the late first century and early second century as the first epistle of John and the letters of Ignatius of Antioch. Of those who adopted such a view are Marcion, Valentinian, and the Manichaeans.[128]

A later Docetic view—first attributed to Basilides by Irenaeus—appeared again in *Sec.*

---

[128] Patricia Crone, "Jewish Christianity and The Qur'an (Part Two)," *Journal of Near Eastern Studies* 75 (2016): 6, doi:10.1086/684957.

Seth. It conveyed that Jesus Christ was not crucified, but rather a substitute—Simon of Cyrene specifically:

> "Those who were there punished me. And I did not die in reality but in appearance, lest I be put to shame by them because these are my kinsfolk. I removed the shame from me and I did not become fainthearted in the face of what happened to me at their hands... For my death, which they think happened, (happened) to them in their error and blindness, since they nailed their man unto their death [...] Yes, they saw me; they punished me. It was another, their father, who drank the gall and the vinegar; it was not I. They struck me with the reed; it was another, Simon, who bore the cross on his shoulder. I was another upon whom they placed the crown of thorns. But I was rejoicing in the height over all the wealth of the archons and the offspring of their error, of their empty glory. And I was laughing at their ignorance."[129]

---

[129] Roger A. Bullard and Joseph A. Gibbons, trans., "The Second Treatise of the Great Seth 9, *The Nag Hammadi Library,* accessed June 3, 2020,

Altering the form, according to the text, seems to be one of the common powers of Jesus that He usually uses, as recounted here:

> "For as I came downward, no one saw me. For I was altering my shapes, changing from form to form. And therefore, when I was at their gates, I assumed their likeness."[130]

The Gnostic principles are clear in the text. It portrays all the great biblical figures of the Old Testament as deluded men because they worshiped another angelic being, the Demiurge, the creator of the world, and not the true God. The text depicts each one of them as a laughingstock when Jesus mentioned them one by one:

> "for Adam was a laughingstock, since he was made a counterfeit type of man by the Hebdomad […] Abraham and Isaac and Jacob were a laughingstock, since they, the counterfeit fathers […] from Adam to Moses and John

---

http://gnosis.org/naghamm/2seth.html.
[130] Ibid., 10.

the Baptist, none of them knew me nor my brothers."[131]

The other Docetic explanation regarded Christ as a divine being that inhabited the man Jesus "proclaimed that the spiritual Jesus departed from his physical counterpart prior to the passion."[132] Jesus was a temporary host for the Divine Christ. This view is adopted by Cerinthus and Carpocrates as mentioned before. The *Gospel of Judas* recounted this belief in Jesus' dialogue with Judas, where Jesus said to Judas, "you will sacrifice the man that clothes me."[133] The man clothes Jesus is a common reference to the physical body that imprisons Him. By betraying Jesus, Judas would do a good favor that will set Christ free from the limitations of the body allowing him to return back to the Pleroma.[134] A similar view also exists in the Coptic *Apocalypse of Peter*:

---

[131] Ibid., 16.
[132] Brown and Griggs, Ibid., 136.
[133] Strathearn, Ibid., 31.
[134] Ibid.

> "Jesus explains that 'his fleshly counterpart' is being nailed to the cross while the 'living' (glorified) Jesus is above the cross laughing at the ignorant folly of the crucifiers."[135]

In the text, Peter saw a vision in which he saw two likenesses of the savior, one is nailed on the cross while the other is free, standing above the cross and laughing.[136] The Docetic elements are obvious in the text. It also contains striking parallels with *Sec. Seth*, such as the "blinding" crucifiers, the "laughing" Jesus, and the "shame" attached to the Crucifixion. However, the identity of the crucified is not Simon as mentioned in *Sec. Seth*, but :

> "his fleshly counterpart, into whose hands and feet they are driving the nails, is the substitute whom they put to shame. He it is who was in his (Jesus') likeness."[137]

---

[135] Brown and Griggs, Ibid.
[136] Ibid., 135.
[137] Ibid., 144.

The physical part of Jesus is treated as a similar substitute to the living Christ who was united with him. He is not a different person as in the case of Simon, but His fleshly part. The two united persons of the same being were separated at the Crucifixion as is recounted in the text:

> "The one who stood near him who was arrested. And he was set free, and he stood joyfully watching those who had taken him by force after they (the spiritual and fleshly Jesus) parted one from another [...] the one who suffers as to the body, therefore, will be the one who is the substitute. And the one who has been set free is my bodiless body."[138]

Finally, there are three major Docetic views on the Crucifixion when observing the texts. Either Jesus seemed to suffer just in appearance as He did not own a real physical body, or He replaced His form with another person who was crucified in His stead (the

---

[138] Ibid., 145.

Substitution Theory), or it was His physical counterpart or the host who received Christ at baptism was crucified but the heavenly Christ has ascended to the Father (the Host Theory). Basilides adopted the second view, but the question is: what made Basilides opt for the Substitution Theory?

Basilides of Alexandria

Basilides was a Gnostic Christian philosopher who was active in Alexandria, Egypt,[139] during the reign of Emperor Hadrian at AD 132-135.[140] He wrote a gospel under his name, but some scholars suggest that it was just a biblical commentary.[141] Bentley Layton argues

---

[139] Bentley Layton, "The Significance of Basilides in Ancient Christian Thought," *Representations*, no. 28 (1989): 149, 150. Layton in the endnote 17 rejects the title "Gnostic" mentioning that it is misleading and throughout his article he considers Basilides a Christian philosopher that bore the thoughts and ideas of many Alexandrian Christian philosophers at his time, who usually embrace elements from Platonism and Stoicism in their thought.
[140] Ibid., 137.
[141] James A. Kelhoffer, "Basilides's Gospel and 'Exegetica (Treatises),'" *Vigiliae Christianae* 59, no. 2 (2005): 116.

that as Constantine in the fourth century declared Orthodox Christianity to be the official religion for the empire,

> "almost all detailed information about alternative philosophies such as that of Basilides perished for lack of official interest; nor has any of Basilides' written works been transmitted by the Byzantine scriptoria."[142]

There is no single surviving work penned by Basilides; we can gather information on his figure from the early Christian writers who wrote against him, namely Irenaeus of Lyons, Clement of Alexandria, Origen of Alexandria, Hippolytus of Rome, and Agrippa Castor.[143] From these five writers, Layton picks Clement to be the most reliable source that he would measure the reliability of other writers based on him. He chose Clement because he was the next generation or two after Basilides, they were historically close, both lived in Alexandria, both were Christian

---

[142] Layton, Ibid., 136.
[143] Ibid., 137.

philosophers, and Clement was interested in Basilides' thought.

Irenaeus owns the earliest account of the doctrines of Basilides which is thought to be based on a lost work of Justin Martyr.[144] Accounts of Basilides, whether in regard to his personal life or his theological thought, have always been disputed because we cannot reconcile all his different accounts that were recorded by all those who wrote about, or rather, against him.[145]

The identity of the teacher of Basilides was disputed too. According to Irenaeus, Basilides was the successor of Simon Magus and Menander and learned from them. However, according to Clement, Basilides himself claimed that he was an apostolic successor and his teacher was Glaukias, the "interpreter" of the apostle Peter. Basilidians claimed that they based their thought on the

---

[144] Antti Marjanen and Petri Luomanen, *A Companion to Second-Century Christian "Heretics"* (Leiden; Boston: Brill, 2008), 2, http://site.ebrary.com/id/10363801.
[145] Ibid., 3.

teachings of apostle Matthias.[146] According to Hippolytus, Basilides and his son, Isidore, claimed that they received secret teachings from the apostle Matthias himself.[147]

All these claims cannot be traced back to Basilides himself. Hippolytus' claims of Basilides are impossible as chronologically, Basilides and the apostle Matthias would have never meet. Hence it is thought of as a distortion of what Clement stated: that the Basilidians basing their thought on Matthias' teachings.[148] Layton was suspicious about Irenaeus' claim of linking Basilides with Menander[149] and supports Basilides' claim about his apostolic succession through Glaukias. However, he agrees that such a supposition is not confirmed by any direct evidence unless Glaukias hailed from Alexandria as well.[150] If we assume this claim to be true, does

---

[146] Ibid., 4.
[147] Ibid.
[148] Ibid.
[149] Layton, Ibid., 137.
[150] Ibid., 146.

it mean that the thoughts of Basilides were transmitted to him from Peter the apostle through Glaukias (i.e. Basilides' thought belonged to Peter in the first place)? To answer this question, we must investigate two entities: the source and the channel. The source in our case would be Peter the apostle, and the channel would be Glaukias through which the supposed Petrine tradition was transmitted to Basilides.

Firstly, it is unlikely that Peter, as a devout Jew, adopted a Gnostic cosmology or believed in Gnostic doctrines, like that of the Demiurge creator, dualistic reality, hostility to matter, or the existence of many gods emanated from the ultimate God. Secondly, Peter certainly believed in the reality of the Crucifixion and the death of Jesus. He confessed to this reality publicly in his famous Acts speech: "you killed the Author of life, whom God raised from the dead. To this we are witnesses."[151] Regarding the specific declaration

---

[151] Acts 3:15

"you killed the Author of Life," George Robert Wynne writes that it is clear that he (Peter) was in possession of truth resting on a higher level than that which is associated with synoptic teaching.[152] Peter was then speaking of something which he truly experienced himself. On another occasion, Peter confessed "the God of our fathers raised Jesus, whom you killed by hanging him on a tree."[153] This confession, along with others in Peter's speeches in Acts,

> "are regarded by the critic as due to a truly primitive source; in other words, which we may believe to represent with considerable accuracy the essential part of what Saint Peter said."[154]

Moreover, the idea of Jesus changing His shape from one form into another more likely belongs to ancient Greek beliefs not Jewish ones;

---

[152] George Robert Wynne, "The Christology of the Petrine Speeches," *The Irish Church Quarterly* 4, no. 16 (1911): 300.
[153] Acts 5:30
[154] Wynne, Ibid., 298.

in Greek mythology, gods change form into other beings via metamorphosis.[155]

As for Glaukias, Layton sees no reason to doubt that Glaukias has earned a reputation as a striking early commentator on Petrine corpus.[156] However, Layton argues that being the interpreter of Peter does not mean that Glaukias accompanied Peter on his apostolic journeys. By examining "Fragment G," a fragment from Book 23 of Basilides' *Commentaries*, Layton elucidated Glaukias' position.[157] Layton discovered that Fragment G is an exegesis of 1 Peter 4: 12-19. Therefore, Basilides wrote an expositor of Peter as an "interpreter of Peter" following his master's work. In that sense, Glaukias can be an interpreter of Peter, a commentator who also can introduce his own views and ideas while interpreting the writings of Peter. This definition of interpreter is different than saying that

---

[155] Prosser, *Was Jesus Crucified?*, 149.
[156] Layton, Ibid., 146.
[157] Ibid.

Glaukias received from Peter himself certain teachings and transmitted them to his disciples. This is unlike the case of Mark the disciple who, according to Papias, "composed his gospel by editing materials transmitted by Peter." [158] It is unlikely that Basilides' beliefs and ideas were received from Peter the apostle.

Henry Longueville Mansel thinks that Basilides is the connecting link between the Syriac form of Gnosticism and the Egyptian form of Gnosticism as he,

> "united in his own teaching the heterogeneous ingredients of the one and the other [...] as belonging in his own person to both countries: Syrian by birth, Egyptian by residence, the disciple of the Samaritan Menander."[159]

Mansel adopted Irenaeus' statement that Basilides was a disciple of Menander and he integrates two types of Gnosticism to create a mixture of teachings.

---

[158] Ibid.
[159] Mansel, Ibid., 144.

August Neander states that:

> "the account of Epiphanius, that Syria, the general birth-place of Gnostic systems, was also the native land of Basilides, is not in itself improbable, although it is on the other hand not a sufficient proof."[160]

According to Neander, Basilides was raised in Syria, the motherland of the Gnostic systems which might has influenced his beliefs however uncertain Neander seems to be about this position.

Walter Bauer agrees that Basilides brought his Gnostic ideas from Antioch as he recounts:

> "Another pupil of Menander, Basilides, is the first of whom we hear that he brought gnostic ideas from Antioch to Alexandria, and thereby took up, from the Christian side, the religious interchange between Egypt and Syria."[161]

---

[160] Neander and Rose, Ibid., 55.
[161] Walter Bauer, *Orthodoxy and Heresy in Earliest Christianity*, eds. Robert A Kraft, and Gerhard Krodel (Mifflintown: Sigler Press, 1996), 62.

It is also worth mentioning that the heretics of Syria-Antioch had access to a gospel that suited their own views. They attributed it to Peter the apostle, and Basilides claimed he received his teachings from Peter through Glaukias.[162] Antioch seemed to be a popular center of Paganism before embracing Christianity. Han J. W. Drijvers describes a few scholarly opinions on early Syria. He states the view of Andreas Feldtkeller on the early Christian missions in Antioch who agrees that,

> "the mission among pagans, of which Antioch was the center, brought Christianity into contact with the various syncretistic Hellenistic religions of antique Syria and produced a multiform Christianity."[163]

This theory, adopted by Mansel, Neander, and Bauer, attributes Basilides' teaching to

---

[162] Ibid.
[163] Han J. W. Drijvers, "Early Syriac Christianity: Some Recent Publications," *Vigiliae Christianae* 50, no. 2 (1996): 159.

Antioch and his discipleship to Menander; it is different than that adopted by Layton, who was suspicious about linking Basilides with Menander and found his discipleship to Glaukias possible if Glaukias was an Alexandrian. The evidence cannot confirm one theory over the other with certainty. The theory of attributing Basilides' discipleship to Menander belongs to Irenaeus, while that attributing his discipleship to Glaukias belongs to Clement of Alexandria. However, as mentioned before, Layton states that there is no direct evidence of the discipleship to Glaukias.

Regarding the beliefs of Basilides, Clement writes that he was an octonaritarian who believed in a godhead of eight divine hypostases which are: un-engendered parent, intellect (Nous), verbal expression (Logos, Word), prudence, wisdom, power, justice, and peace.[164] Neander translated the names of some of these hypostases with slight

---

[164] Layton, Ibid., 138. The word hypostases is used here because these seven qualities that emanates from the sourceless source are not abstract qualities but living, personified powers.

differences, so instead of prudence, he named it thought, and instead of justice, he named it holiness or moral perfection.[165] The unengendered parent is the sourceless source from which emanates all the other seven hypostases in successive order. God created the materialistic universe through the wisdom hypostasis—who work as an agent for God—along with some angels.[166] The created universe consists of 365 heavens formed as nested spheres, each sphere embraces the other innermost spheres, and the Earth and its sky is the innermost center of them all. These heavens are expressed by the mystical Greek word "Abraxas" or sometimes "Abrasax" [Greek: ΑΒΡΑΞΑΣ] as each letter when translated to its numerical value based on the Greek system will result in the number 365.[167] Out and apart of all these spheres are God and His seven

---

[165] Neander and Rose, Ibid.
[166] Layton, Ibid., 142.
[167] Neander and Rose, Ibid., 56. [A = 1 + B = 2 + P = 100 + A = 1 + Ξ = 60 + A = 1 + Σ = 200 = 365] Abraxas also was a symbol of the Basilidians.

hypostases so that He contains all but contained by nothing.[168] Each sphere is motivated by a certain superior angel who created and governs it, and the creator angel of the 365th innermost heaven (and Earth) is the god of Israel whom they worship, while every other nation worships one of the other angels who helped God in creation.[169] Figure 1 presents Basilides' cosmology based on this explanation.

The dualistic view of Basilides divides between Light and Darkness, Life and Death, Soul and Matter, Good and Evil.[170] These opposing elements exist in the form of intermixtures of one another throughout the whole course of the universe. These intermixtures were formed when Darkness and Death attach themselves to the fallen seed of Light and Life, Evil attaches itself to Good, and the un-Divine to the Divine, without causing damage to the original being.[171] It is just

---

[168] Layton, Ibid.
[169] Ibid., 143.
[170] Neander and Rose, Ibid., 57.
[171] Ibid., 58.

like rust when it falls on iron and attaches itself to it. So as the rusted iron should enter a cleaning process to return to its original state, the intermixture of Light and Darkness should enter a purification process for the seed of Light to be purified from everything foreign to it.[172] This is the case for everything that exists, not only man, but even stones, plants, and animals. All nature contains life which is held prisoner by matter, with different degrees of imprisonmen, and strive to set itself free through gradual stages of development, from stone to plant, then to animal, and lastly to human, in an evolutionary manner.[173]

---

[172] Ibid.
[173] Ibid., 59.

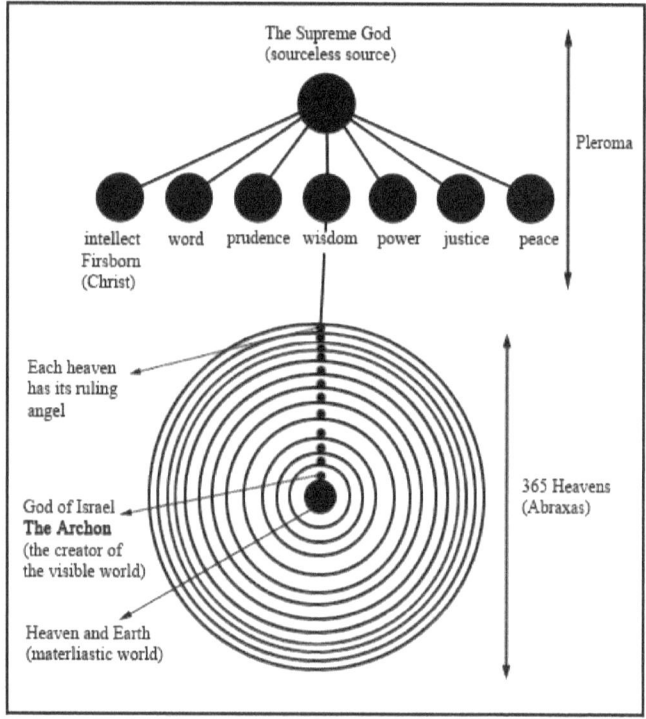

Figure 1: Basilides Cosmology

Basilides did not consider the creator god, also called the Ruler (Archon), an evil being as he did not govern the visible world independent from the true God, but was guided by Him. The creator god was not conscious of this fact and was unaware of the higher spiritual levels above him, unlike the common Gnostic view which portrays the creator archon as an evil demiurge.[174] This led, at some point in time and out of ignorance, to believe that he was the supreme God, unaware of the existence of the true supreme God.[175] According to Layton, a disaster happened when the creator Archon, the god of Israel, tried to subordinate all other nations to Israel, so the true God, the ultimate sourceless parent, sent Christ, his first hypostases, to save the world as Jesus the Messiah.[176]

Basilides viewed Christ as the first hypostases (the intellect) that emanates from the sourceless parent and came to the Earth for a mission of salvation. Neander supports that Basilides did not believe that Jesus Christ was a God-man redeemer who inseparably united divinity and humanity, but He was only an instrument who the Supreme God chose to send His firstborn son, the Nous, to "reveal Himself in

---

[174] Ibid., 60.
[175] Ibid., 63.
[176] Layton, Ibid., 144.

human nature, and to seize on that nature so as to work upon it."[177] Then, Christ united Himself with the man Jesus at his baptism from which He started His redeeming task by speaking extraordinary things that were far beyond the reach of the lower creation to illuminate all those elect of spiritual nature and elevate them above the materialistic world, the man Jesus included.[178] There is a dispute among scholars regarding the Substitution Theory of Basilides. Neander argues that Basilides adopted the same idea of Cerinthus, holding that Christ, after completing His redemptive mission, left the body of Jesus at the time of the Crucifixion and ascended to the Pleroma, leaving Jesus to experience the suffering that does not have any role in the redeeming process.[179] Mansel, as well, thinks that Basilides did not adopt the Substitution Theory, basing his opinion on Hippolytus. Hippolytus acknowledged

---

[177] Neander and Rose, Ibid., 63.
[178] Ibid.
[179] Ibid., 65.

that the disciples of Basilides accepted the Gospel narratives and the reality of Jesus' sufferings, but it was only intended to separate the spiritual component in the universe from the foreign inferior components of the materialistic world which were mixed with it. Jesus was the first fruit of this separation, and as such, the sufferings resulted in disintegrating His bodily component into formlessness and His other components ascended each one to its corresponding realm: the psychical to the realm of the great Archon; the spiritual to the spiritual region of the spirit; and the divine to the Pleroma.[180] Mansel bases his opinion on Hippolytus:

> "From this statement of Hippolytus, which is indirectly confirmed by Clement of Alexandria, it appears that Basilides did not adopt the Docetic views of the person of Jesus which were attributed to him (or perhaps rather to his followers) by Irenaeus and others. Especially that strange and profane fancy, that Simon of Cyrene was changed into

---

[180] Mansel, Ibid., 157.

> the likeness of Jesus and suffered in his stead, while Jesus, in the form of Simon, stood by and laughed at his enemies, could have had no place in the original teaching of Basilides, though it may have been engrafted on his system by some of its later exponents."[181]

On the other hand, Layton attributes the Substitution Theory to Basilides and synthesizes a reasonable justification for his claim about the Crucifixion. Since Basilides believes that Christ is the preexistent first hypostatic emanation of the source-less parent and lives in the realm of gods outside the created universe, therefore His appearance on Earth would not require real change into matter, so He appeared as a spiritual incorporeal power. He was incapable to suffer in a physical sense; although this is inconsistent with what truly happened, the Crucifixion of Jesus was of the flesh, of real pain and death as the New Testament gospels portray.[182] So Basilides then

---

[181] Ibid.
[182] Layton, Ibid., 144.

came up with a solution to compromise his view with the biblical narratives:

> "the first hypostasis (Jesus) had transformed its manifestation into the form of Simon of Cyrene, and Simon into the form of Jesus. Thus, one might say, formally Jesus Christ was crucified, but substantially He was not."[183]

The actual person who truly suffered and died on the cross is Simon of Cyrene, not Christ. Robert M. Grant, attributing the theory to Basilides' followers, thinks that since the Basilidians do not believe that Christ was truly incarnated so they have developed this idea of exchanging the form between Christ and Simon as an explanation for the story of the Crucifixion.[184] Neander too attributes the same construction of the theory to the Basilidians. Christ, as a redeeming spirit, could not connect with the Demiurge's matter, so He took upon himself only

---

[183] Ibid., 145.
[184] Robert M. Grant, "Gnostic Origins and the Basilidians of Irenaeus," *Vigiliae Christianae* 13, no. 2 (1959): 123.

an appearance of a physical body. However, when the Jews managed to crucify him, He took the form of Simon as He can clothe himself in any kind of bodily appearance, and He made Simon appear in his likeness as an illusion before the blind multitude of Jews. Then He raised himself up into the spiritual world while mocking those who were deluded.[185] Scholars like Winrich Alfried Löhr, Neander, Grant, and Mansel suggest that the crucifixion part was a later addition by Basilides' followers,[186] whereas Layton agrees that it was founded by Basilides himself, "Basilides assumes that Jesus was never substantially crucified, as Irenaeus tells us."[187]

Layton noticed the common theme of Basilides' theology and his biblical interpretations are "anti-Jewish and perhaps Docetist in his reading of the biblical text."[188] Basilides might have based his theory on a literal

---

[185] Neander and Rose, Ibid., 105.
[186] Kelhoffer, Ibid., 119.
[187] Layton, Ibid., 140.
[188] Ibid., 145.

interpretation of Mark 15 as it mentions the following:[189]

> "And they compelled a passerby, Simon of Cyrene, who was coming in from the country, the father of Alexander and Rufus, to carry his cross. And they brought him to the place called Golgotha (which means Place of a Skull). And they offered him wine mixed with myrrh, but he did not take it. And they crucified him and divided his garments among them, casting lots for them, to decide what each should take."[190]

The Docetic interpretation may find solid ground in the literal reading of the previous passage. Although the sequence of events shows an ambiguity toward the identity of the crucified, as the phrase "and they brought him" might refer also to Simon, we must take this passage out of context to interpret it as it was for Simon. In the previous chapter, Jesus predicted His death more

---

[189] Grant, Ibid.
[190] Mark 15:21-24

than once. The first prediction is when He defended the woman who poured the ointment of pure nard over His head saying, "she has done what she could; she has anointed my body beforehand for burial."[191] The second prediction is during the Last Supper, Jesus said, "this is my blood of the covenant, which is poured out for many."[192] Speaking of His burial and His poured blood can neither signify His escape nor any intention of such.

Hence the Substitution Theory was invented, either by Basilides or his followers, as a result of their beliefs regarding the appearance of Jesus on Earth as an incorporeal spirit, along with the historical fact that someone was truly crucified under the name of Jesus. The Orthodox Fathers responded to these claims when this interpretation came to the surface; they were already fighting against different forms Docetism even before it officially appeared.

---

[191] Mark 14:8
[192] Mark 14:24

The Orthodox Response to the Theory

Gnostics held Docetism as doctrine along with other beliefs that were foreign to the Gospel, yet they claimed that they have received such teachings from Christ and His apostles.[193] They managed to prove such a claim by imposing their ready-formed theosophic system on the biblical texts, as Neander notes "they went to the Holy Scriptures, and sought to find in them something to hang their system upon."[194] Neander states that they could achieve that easily but at the cost of falling into grammatical errors and illogical interpretations. On the other hand, their opponents—the Orthodox—sought to establish a more accurate grammatical and logical interpretation of the Bible.[195] The Orthodox Church had to prove herself the sole keeper of the truth. She discussed the sources and criteria of her teachings in defending Christian doctrine. She

---

[193] Neander and Rose, Ibid., 44.
[194] Ibid.
[195] Ibid., 45.

stood against Gnostic teachings on the unity of God and the doctrine of salvation and redemption.[196] The Orthodox bishops and councils wrote apologetic writings to explain, defend, and prove the truth of their doctrines and to expose whatever heretical teachings appeared. They also sent pastoral letters to believers to warn them about wrong teachings and Gnostic views. This was no easy task for the Church. Walker mentions that the influence of Gnosticism in the second century was strong and its ideas were spreading so rapidly, that it threatened to overwhelm the historic Christian faith, and by so doing, brought the Christian Church its gravest crisis.[197]

The earliest and most popular passages that seem to be directed against Docetism can be found in I John, where John relates:

> "That which was from the beginning, which we have heard, which we have seen with our eyes,

---

[196] Malaty, Ibid., 26.
[197] Walker et al., Ibid., 53.

> which we looked upon and have touched with our hands, concerning the word of life—the life was made manifest, and we have seen it, and testify to it."[198]

John is providing direct, sensible evidence of an eyewitness and personal friend to prove the reality of the human body in which his master assumed on Earth.[199] John continues to announce in plain language that,

> "every spirit that confesses that Jesus Christ has come in the flesh is from God, and every spirit that does not confess Jesus is not from God. This is the spirit of the antichrist, which you heard was coming and now is in the world already."[200]

John here uses his personal experience to refute Docetic claims that Jesus was an incorporeal spirit.

In Ignatius' *Epistle to the Smyrnaeans*, he warns his Church not to accept Docetic beliefs. He

---

[198] 1 John 1:1
[199] Mansel, Ibid., 76.
[200] 1 John 4:1-3

links the suffering of Christ with our salvation stating that,

> "He (Christ) suffered all these things for our sakes, that we might be saved. And He suffered truly, even as also He truly raised up Himself, not, as certain unbelievers maintain, that He only seemed to suffer."[201]

Denying the reality of Jesus' suffering is rejecting His salvation. Ignatius also refers to the Scriptures to prove his Orthodox position:

> "When, for instance, He (Jesus) came to those who were with Peter, He said to them, 'Lay hold, handle Me, and see that I am not an incorporeal spirit.'[202] And

---

[201] Ignatius of Antioch, *The Epistle of Ignatius to the Smyrnaeans* 2, *Ante-Nicene Fathers: The Writings of the Fathers Down to A.D. 325*, Vol. 1. Eds. A.C. Coxe, J. Donaldson, A. Roberts, (Grand Rapids: Eerdmans Publishing, 1989), 87.

[202] Luke 24:39: "See my hands and my feet, that it is I myself. Touch me and see. For a spirit does not have flesh and bones as you see that I have." It seems that Ignatius was using the Gospel of Luke but a short version of the verse. This shows that the Gospel of Luke was authoritative to the Orthodox Christians and most probably to the docetae too if we considered that this response was directed to them or used to refute their claims.

immediately they touched Him, and believed, being convinced both by His flesh and spirit. For this cause also they despised death and were found its conquerors. And after his resurrection He ate and drank with them, as being possessed of flesh."[203]

Ignatius here provides biblical evidence of Jesus referring to His body as real and physical, not as a ghost-like spirit. Moreover, he adds the martyrdom of the disciples as additional evidence; the driving motive for their martyrdom was Jesus' own true suffering, death, and resurrection, which made them courageously face death. He stresses on the Scriptures as a significant proof of Christ's real suffering, and he also guides his Church to pay attention to the Scriptures in this matter:

"Give heed to the prophets, and above all, to the Gospel, in which

---

[203] Ignatius of Antioch, *The Epistle of Ignatius to the Smyrnaeans* 3, *Ante-Nicene Fathers: The Writings of the Fathers Down to A.D. 325*, Vol. 1. Eds. A.C. Coxe, J. Donaldson, A. Roberts, (Grand Rapids: Eerdmans Publishing, 1989), 87.

the passion [of Christ] has been revealed to us, and the resurrection has been fully proved."[204]

It is understood from Ignatius' defense that he did not encounter the Substitution Theory, as he never mentioned anything about the identity of the crucified. He only encountered those who believed "that He only seemed to suffer."[205] It seems that the Substitution Theory was not yet developed during his lifetime. All that Ignatius tried to prove is that Christ possessed a real physical body and experienced real suffering on the cross.[206]

Polycarp, one of the Apostolic Fathers, seems to be writing against the Docetae in his *Epistle to the Philippians*:

---

[204] Ibid., chap. 7.
[205] Ignatius of Antioch, *The Epistle of Ignatius to the Trallians* 10, *Ante-Nicene Fathers: The Writings of the Fathers Down to A.D. 325, Vol. 1.* Eds. A.C. Coxe, J. Donaldson, A. Roberts, (Grand Rapids: Eerdmans Publishing, 1989), 70.
[206] Ignatius of Antioch, *The Epistle of Ignatius to the Smyrnaeans* 1, *Ante-Nicene Fathers: The Writings of the Fathers Down to A.D. 325, Vol. 1.* Eds. A.C. Coxe, J. Donaldson, A. Roberts, (Grand Rapids: Eerdmans Publishing, 1989), 86.

"For whosoever does not confess that Jesus Christ has come in the flesh, is antichrist; and whosoever does not confess the testimony of the cross, is of the devil [...] Wherefore, forsaking the vanity of many, and their false doctrines, let us return to the word which has been handed down to us from the beginning."[207]

Polycarp here defends his position by holding on to the original teachings that were handed down to Christians, admitting that the Docetic teachings are neither original nor handed down by an apostolic source. It is most likely that Polycarp received these teachings directly from the apostle John, since he was John's disciple.[208]

As discussed earlier, the Gnostics divided mankind into categories according to their capacity for enlightenment and their eligibility for

---

[207] Polycarp of Smyrna, *The Epistle of Polycarp to the Philippians* 7, A *Ante-Nicene Fathers: The Writings of the Fathers Down to A.D. 325*, Vol. 1. Eds. A.C. Coxe, J. Donaldson, A. Roberts, (Grand Rapids: Eerdmans Publishing, 1989), 34.
[208] Malaty, Ibid., 8.

salvation. They attributed such an idea of categorization to Jesus and His apostles. They claimed that Jesus and His apostles taught each man according to his ability. To the blind and ignorant, they taught only of the Demiurge's teachings as they could not understand anything higher; to those of spiritual nature, they communicated an esoteric knowledge of the Pleroma, circulated orally and secretly among a small circle.[209] Irenaeus, in his seminal work, *Against Heresies* (182-188),[210] responds to this opinion by responding that if the apostles truly taught their doctrines according to the capacity of their hearers and gave answers that suit the opinions of their questioners, it would be like teaching blind things to the blind who think of the Demiurge and truthful things to those who were capable to comprehend the unnamable Father, then "the Lord and the apostles exercised the office of teacher not to further the cause of truth,

---

[209] Neander and Rose, Ibid., 45.
[210] Mansel, Ibid., 240.

but even in hypocrisy, and as each individual was able to receive it!"[211] He also finds that this claim contradicts the simple message of Jesus, who came as the physician of the sick and called the sinners to repentance for, "what medical man, anxious to heal a sick person, would prescribe in accordance with the patient's whims, and not according to the requisite medicine?"[212] The apostles were assigned to give sight to those who saw not, and medicine to the weak, they certainly did not speak to them according to their blind opinions, but according to the "revealed truth" that leads to salvation,

> "for no persons of any kind would act properly, if they should advise blind men, just about to fall over a precipice, to continue their most dangerous path, as if it were the

---

[211] Irenaeus of Lyons, *Against Heresies* 3.5.1, *Ante-Nicene Fathers: The Writings of the Fathers Down to A.D. 325, Vol. 1.* Eds. A.C. Coxe, J. Donaldson, A. Roberts, (Grand Rapids: Eerdmans Publishing, 1989), 418.

[212] Ibid.

right one, and as if they might go on in safety." [213]

Clement of Alexandria, the theologian of the late second and early third centuries,[214] refutes the moral and practical sides of the Gnostic teachings, such as their denial of free will and their rejection of marriage as a consequence of their hostility to the physical world.[215] He refutes the main Gnostic doctrines indirectly by explaining the definition of the true Gnostic or perfect Christian against that defined by the Gnostic sects.[216] He also explains the Christian view towards matter versus the Gnostic view that considered material evil. He teaches that the body is fitted for the contemplation of heaven, its senses participate in acquiring knowledge, it is the habitation of the precious human soul, and it is thought worthy of the Holy Spirit.[217] However,

---

[213] Ibid.
[214] Mansel, Ibid., 261.
[215] Ibid., 264.
[216] Ibid., 270.
[217] Ibid., 268.

Orthodox Christianity stands against the wrongdoings and the deviated desires of the body, but not the body itself as Paul states, "for the desires of the flesh are against the Spirit, and the desires of the Spirit are against the flesh."[218] "The body is not bad by nature" explains why Orthodox Christians accept the real, true incarnation of Christ while Gnostic Christians do not.[219]

Hippolytus of Rome is another apologist who refutes Gnostic doctrines using historical methods. He traced their principles historically to prove that the Gnostics borrowed their doctrines from heathen sources and that was enough to demonstrate that the "theories which the heretics put forth as of Divine inspiration are really stolen from the inventions of heathen men."[220]

---

[218] Galatians 5:17
[219] Mansel, Ibid.
[220] Ibid., 275.

Islam and Gnosticism

Overview of Islamic Theology

Islam emerged in the Arabian Peninsula in AD 610 when Muhammad believed to have received his first divine revelation.[221] Muhammad the Prophet, is the founder of Islam who, according to Muslim sources, received revelations from God as individual verses, which he then dictated to his followers and eventually formed the Qu'ran.[222]

---

[221] A. Schimmel, *And Muhammad Is His Messenger: The Veneration of the Prophet in Islamic Piety*, (Chapel Hill: University of North Carolina Press, 2014).
[222] Gerhard Endress and Carole Hillenbrand, *Islam: An Historical Introduction* (New Delhi: New Age Books, 2006), 22.

The Qu'ran, according to Muslims, is the Word of God, the revelation to mankind in which God reveals His divinity and His command to men.[223] The name of God in Islam is *Allah*, his essential personal name.[224] Islam is an Arabic word which means submission, that is, the complete trust in and acknowledgment of the one, supreme God.[225]

The articles of faith are the major beliefs that a person should believe to become Muslim. The first and most important article of faith is the belief in the absolute unity of God [*tawhid*] in a strict sense.[226] This is expressed by the statement "There is no deity but Allah" [*La ilaha illallah*]. This statement, along with the confession that Muhammed is a prophet of Allah, forms the foundational creed of Islam.[227] Allah is the Creator, Designer, Controller, and the Governor of the universe. He is described as "Infinite and

---

[223] Ibid.
[224] Sayyid Abul A'la Mawdudi, *Towards Understanding Islam,* (Leicestershire: The Islamic Foundation, 2013), 46.
[225] Schimmel, Ibid.
[226] Mawdudi, Ibid., 45,
[227] Ibid, 44.

Eternal, All-Powerful, All-Wise, Omnipotent and Omniscient, All-knowing and All-Seeing."[228] The second article is to believe in Angels, immaterial beings that cannot be seen by physical eyes,

> "who are believed to be engaged in the administration of the universe; for instance, one controls the air, another imparts light, another brings rain, and so on [...] and they have no share in God's divinity."[229]

The third article is to believe in the books which Allah has sent down to mankind through His prophets.[230] Islam confirms that Allah sent down Books through prophets as the Torah of Moses, the Psalms (*Zabur*) of David, and the Gospel (*Injil*) of Jesus Christ, and the last one is the Qu'ran. Muslims believe that these Books were revealed the same way as the Qu'ran was revealed.[231] Muslims believe that such books were truly from God, and yet they believe that

---

[228] Ibid., 49.
[229] Ibid., 54.
[230] Ibid., 55.
[231] Ibid., 56.

they were extinct and the current scriptures with Christians and Jews are corrupt, changed, and altered throughout the centuries.[232] Only the Qu'ran was kept preserved unchanged.[233] The fourth article is to believe in God's Prophets that were chosen among every nation.[234] According to the Islamic tradition, there were a total of 124,000 prophets raised by Allah throughout history.[235] The fifth and last article is to believe in life after death.[236] That is to believe in the resurrection and in the day of judgment when all human beings who lived on earth since life begins will be judged before Allah.

Jesus in Islam

Beliefs about Jesus in Islam emerge from a combination of a wide spectrum of thought, from Jewish Christianity to Gnostic Christianity. This

---

[232] Ibid.
[233] Ibid., 57.
[234] Ibid., 60.
[235] Ibid.
[236] Ibid., 63.

somehow confuses Christians when they attempt to understand the identity of the Islamic Jesus. The Islamic Jesus mainly belongs to Jewish Christianity. He is only a human prophet sent to the Israelites like all other prophets, a second in significance to Moses, and one who confirms the Torah.[237]

In Islam, Jesus is called *'Isa*. The Qu'ran refers to Jesus as "the son of Mary because of his virgin birth, as the Messiah, as a messenger of God, as a prophet, as a word from God, and as a spirit from God."[238] Jesus spoke His prophetic role in His cradle after He was born saying:

> "I am indeed a servant of Allah: He hath given me revelation and made me a prophet, and He hath made me blessed wheresoever I be, and hath enjoined on me Prayer and Charity as long as I live."[239]

---

[237] Crone, Ibid., 229.
[238] A. H. Mathias Zahniser, *The Mission and Death of Jesus in Islam and Christianity*. (Eugene: Wipf and Stock Publishers, 2017), 7.
[239] Qu'ran 19:30-31 Youssef Ali.

The prophetic role of Jesus is clear and straightforward: God made Him a prophet and gave Him a revelation to reveal to the people. However, the Qu'ran is unclear regarding some other titles which are designated to Jesus such as when the Qu'ran calls Him:

> "Christ Jesus the son of Mary was (no more than) a messenger of Allah, and His Word [*kalematoh*], which He bestowed on Mary, and a spirit proceeding from Him [*roh menhu*]: so, believe in Allah and His messengers."[240]

It designates Jesus as Christ (the Messiah), a messenger of Allah, His Word, and a Spirit proceeding from Him. The question remains: in what sense Jesus is the Christ or the Word of God? Here the sort of confusion that I mentioned earlier persists. Patricia Crone states:

> "although he calls him *al-Masih* (Christ) and *al-Kalima* (the Word), he does not credit Jesus with the characteristic features of the Christian messiah or present him

---

[240] Qu'ran 4:171 Youssef Ali.

as the Logos in the Christian sense."[241]

For Christians, the Messiah is the anointed one who has a sacrificial role to redeem the world and He is a king of David's descendants; in contrast to the Qu'ran, Jesus has neither sacrificial nor redemptive role, He was never called a king, and was presented as a descendant of Aaron rather than David.[242] The term "Christ" even caused some confusion among Muslim scholars. Al-Tabari, one of the earliest Sunni Muslim scholars, stated that the origin of the word Christ is he who is wiped [*asl Al-Masih: Al-Mamsooh*], and God labeled Him as such because God has wiped Him from His sins [*samah Allah bezalek letat-heeroh eyah mn al-zenoob*].[243] Al-Tobrosi, a Shiite Muslim scholar, adds another meaning to

---

[241] Crone, Ibid.
[242] Crone, Ibid., 19.
[243] Tafsir Al-Tabari, "Altafsir.Com - The Tafsirs," v. Q 4:171, accessed June 26, 2020,
https://www.altafsir.com/Tafasir.asp?tMadhNo=1&tTafsirNo=1&tSoraNo=4&tAyahNo=171&tDisplay=yes&Page=1&Size=1&LanguageId=1.

the term that he heard from an unknown source that Jesus was called the Messiah because He used to wipe the earth walking [*kan yamsah al-ard mashyan*].[244] The messianic role of Christ is not present in the Qu'ran, and the term "Christ" has no implications in the Islamic thought and has nothing to do with the Christian understanding of it, as Crone recounts, "He was the messiah only in the sense that this is what everyone called Him, perhaps already in pre-Islamic Arabia."[245]

In regard to the term "God's Word" [*kalematoh*], or in the Christian terminology, "the Logos," Christians with their different denominations understand it as a divine being who existed before the creation of the world and by which God created the world. The Jewish Christian sects who regarded Jesus as a wholly

---

[244] Tafsir Al-Tobrosi, "Altafsir.Com - The Tafsirs," v. Q 4:171, accessed June 26, 2020, https://www.altafsir.com/Tafasir.asp?tMadhNo=0&tTafsirNo=3&tSoraNo=4&tAyahNo=171&tDisplay=yes&UserProfile=0&LanguageId=1.
[245] Crone, Ibid., 19.

human prophet refused to call Him the Logos.[246] It is inconsistent to call Jesus "the Word of God" while considering Him merely human. Although the meaning of the term is not present in the Qu'ran, as is the case of the term "Christ," commentators attempted to interpret "Logos," crafting two major interpretations. Al-Tabari, in his commentary, explains that the Word of God either means "the annunciation" or the message that God has sent to Mary through His angels [*al-resala allaty amar Allah malaa'ekatoh an taa'ty Mariam beha*], or it means the word "be" by which God has created Jesus in the womb of Mary [*howa kawloh: kon fa kan*].[247]

Many Qu'ranic verses portray Jesus as a prophet sent only to the Israelites, His own people.[248] This view is foreign to mainstream

---

[246] Ibid., 20.
[247] Tafsir Al-Tabari, "Altafsir.Com - The Tafsirs," v. Q 4:171, accessed June 26, 2020,
https://www.altafsir.com/Tafasir.asp?tMadhNo=0&tTafsirNo=1&tSoraNo=4&tAyahNo=171&tDisplay=yes&Page=2&Size=1&LanguageId=1
[248] Crone, Ibid., 229. The Qu'ran depicts Jesus as a messenger to the Israelites as when the angels announce to

Christianity, whether of today or the seventh century Melkites and Jacobites or even the heretical group, the Nestorians.[249] It localizes the message of Christ, yet the canonical gospels report otherwise: Jesus used to cure Gentiles,[250] He asked His disciples to make disciples of all nations and to baptize them,[251] and Gentiles as well as Jews have embraced Christianity from the very first century,[252] which makes the message of Christ universal in the awareness of the mainstream Christians. However, a paradox seems to appear in a certain passage in the Qu'ran that indicates the universalism of Christ when it mentions that Jesus and His mother were a sign

---

Mary the birth of Christ they said that Allah: "(appoint him) a messenger to the Children of Israel, (with this message): I have come to you, with a Sign from your Lord..." (Qu'ran 3:49 Youssef Ali); also "And remember, Jesus, the son of Mary, said: O Children of Israel! I am the messenger of Allah (sent) to you, confirming the Law (which came) before me..." (Qu'ran 61:6 Youssef Ali).
[249] Ibid., 230.
[250] Matthew 8:5-13; Luke 7:1-10.
[251] Matthew 28:19.
[252] Acts 6.

for all peoples[253] and in Sahih International translation "a sign for the worlds" [*aya lil-alamin*].[254]

Islamic View on the Crucifixion

Islam adopts a Docetic view of the Crucifixion based on a single Qu'ranic verse, termed the "denial verse" by Kenneth E. Nolin; this single verse conveys the Illusion doctrine.[255] It states in *Surat Al-Nisaa'*:

> "That they said (in boast), 'We killed Christ Jesus the son of Mary, the Messenger of Allah' but they killed him not, nor crucified him, but so it was made to appear to them... for of a surety they killed him not, Nay, Allah raised him up unto Himself; and Allah is Exalted in Power, Wise."[256]

---

[253] Qu'ran 21:91 Youssef Ali.
[254] Crone, Ibid.
[255] Zahniser, Ibid., 23. Kenneth E. Nolin was a pastor in the Presbyterian Church. He pursued Arabic and Islamic studies, earning an M.A. and later a Ph.D. at the Hartford Seminary Foundation, and encouraged the dialogue and understanding between Christians and Muslims.
[256] Qu'ran 4:157,158 Youssef Ali.

The verse denies the Crucifixion of Jesus, admitting that God has saved Him and raised Him to heaven, and it lacks important information regarding what really happened. Brent Neely offers the following comments on this verse: "it is also important to realize that upon closer examination, the actual language in the Arabic of 4.157 turns out to be anything but obvious or clear."[257] A. H. Mathias Zahniser describes the phrase "it was made to appear to them" [*Shubbeh lahom*] as ambiguous, stating that without commentary readers can never know "who made what look to the Jews as though they had crucified and killed Jesus."[258] The Arabic word [*Shubbeh lahom*] may indicate that someone "seemed for them to be in his (Jesus') likeness" as shown in another Qu'ranic translation "but [another] was made to resemble him to them."[259] However,

---

[257] Brent Neely, "At Cross Purposes: Islam and the Crucifixion of Christ, a Theological Response," *Transformation Transformation: An International Journal of Holistic Mission Studies* 34, no. 3 (2017): 3.
[258] Zahniser, Ibid., 16.
[259] Qu'ran 4: 157, Sahih International.

since the verb is in the passive form (was made to appear/ resemble), Zahniser questions all the possibilities that all seem to be compatible with the passive construction of the verb:

> "Was the event made to look like a crucifixion and killing of Jesus, while in fact he did not really die and was not really crucified? If so, who made it happen thus? Did the Jews think they were the instrumental cause of Jesus' crucifixion and death? [...] Was the person crucified made to look like Jesus? Did he just happen to look like Jesus?"[260]

Since there are unanswered questions, we ought to turn to Islamic commentaries for answers. The lack of information opens the door for many proposed stories narrated in Islamic commentaries, but the dominant view revolves around the Substitution Theory.[261] I will mainly present the ideas of two respected Islamic scholars in the Muslim world, Al-Tabari (d.

---

[260] Ibid., 17.
[261] Neely, Ibid., 12.

923),[262] and Ibn-Kathir (d. 1300),[263] to gain an understanding of how Muslim scholars sought to solve the mystery of the denial verse.

Al-Tabari's commentary is the earliest commentary on the Qu'ran where he,

> "gathers the traditions and hadiths related to each verse, thus providing a window into how the Prophet and Companions and Followers may have interpreted the text."[264]

Joseph L. Cumming summarizes the discourse of Al-Tabari, mentioning that the commentary shows two main stories of the Crucifixion, narrated with variations of details, but both are based on the Substitution Theory.[265]

---

[262] Joseph L. Cumming, "Did Jesus Die on the Cross? The History of Reflection on the End of His Earthly Life in Sunni Tafsir Literature," 2001, 7.
[263] "Ibn Kathīr | Muslim Scholar | Britannica," para. 1, accessed June 26, 2020,
https://www.britannica.com/biography/Ibn-Kathir.
[264] Cumming, Ibid., 7.
[265] Ibid., 10. Joseph L. Cumming is a scholar of Islamic and Christian thought who serves as pastor of the International Church at Yale University and works internationally as a consultant on Muslim-Christian and Muslim-Christian-Jewish relations. Cumming has published numerous articles

The first story supposes that the appearance of Jesus fell upon all of His disciples so that the Jews could not determine the real Jesus, while the second story assumes that Jesus asked for a single volunteer to receive His likeness and be crucified in His stead. In most of the stories, this crucified man is rewarded by accompanying Jesus in paradise. Al-Tabari prefers the idea that the appearance fell upon all of Jesus' disciples which caused the disciples too to get confused, which justifies why the Christians—as they received their faith from the disciples—also got confused, whereas, according to Al-Tabari, if it was a single volunteer then every Christian would be confirming the substitution without confusion or doubt.[266]

Ibn-Kathir, a leading Muslim theologian and historian, in his commentary of the denial verse, tend to rely on a *hadith* narrated by Ibn-

---

on issues affecting relations among the Abrahamic faith communities. He has lectured in Arabic at Al-Azhar University and other Islamic institutions.
[266] Ibid.

Abbas which states that the Jews went to the king of Damascus at the time of Jesus, and they accused Him of stirring the people in Jerusalem against the king. The king then angrily sent his deputy with some Jews to arrest Jesus. When they approached the house where Jesus resided with his companions, Jesus asked his companions,

> "'Who volunteers to be made to look like me, for which he will be my companion in Paradise' A young man volunteered, but Isa (Jesus) thought that he was too young. He asked the question a second and third time, each time the young man volunteering, prompting Isa to say, 'Well then, you will be that man.' Allah made the young man look exactly like Isa, while a hole opened in the roof of the house, and Isa was made to sleep and ascended to heaven while asleep."[267] Then they crucified the guy who likened

---

[267] Ṣafī al-Raḥmān Mubārakfūrī and Ismā'īl ibn 'Umar Ibn Kathīr, *Tafsir ibn Kathir: (abridged)* (Riyadh: Darussalam, 2000), 1202. Ibn-Abbas 'Abd Allāh ibn al-'Abbās, also called Ibn Abbās', a Companion of the prophet Muhammad, one of the greatest scholars of early Islam, and the first exegete of the Qu'ran.

Jesus. This story is similar to the one that Al-Tabari did not prefer.

Although the denial verse describes the Crucifixion, it does not treat the Crucifixion itself and its significance for Christians. It was directed against the Jewish claims and not the Christians, as the word "they said" at the beginning of the verse refers to the Jews in its textual context.[268] That is why some scholars argue that the denial verse, if interpreted in a broader context, is not intended to reject the Crucifixion, but to defend Jesus against the Jewish claims, as the Jews thought they have won by crucifying Jesus. But whether or not Jesus died is simply not the matter at hand.[269] This view seems to be the weakest as it stands against the simple and literal sense of the verse along with the consensus of the Qu'ranic commentaries that deny the Crucifixion.

Interestingly, few Muslim scholars find the Substitution Theory problematic. Al-Ghazali, a

---

[268] Zahniser, Ibid., 23.
[269] Lanier, Ibid.

prominent Muslim theologian and philosopher, argues that if we accept that God changes likeness between humans, then we cannot guarantee that whoever we are dealing with is the same person we know and not someone of his likeness. Following the implicit logic of Al-Ghazalı's discussion, the Christian error over the Crucifixion is based on an innocent mistake, rather than on a conspiracy to defraud.[270] Mahmoud Ayoub, a modern Muslim scholar, finds the Substitution Theory ethically problematic as

> "it makes a mockery of divine justice and the primordial covenant of God with humanity, to guide human history to its final fulfillment. Would it be in consonance with God's covenant, his mercy and justice, to deceive humanity for so many centuries? [...] it makes historical Christianity based on a divine deception which

---

[270] Martin Whittingham, "How Could So Many Christians Be Wrong? The Role of Tawātur (Recurrent Transmission of Reports) in Understanding Muslim Views of the Crucifixion," *Islam and Christian-Muslim Relations* 19, no. 2 (2008): 173.

was not disclosed until the Qu'ran was revealed centuries later."[271]

Neely agrees with this opinion as it is hardly complimentary towards God that He should concoct a sleight-of-hand on the cross whereby a deception spawns an enduring faith community, Christianity.[272] Neely and Ayoub contend that if Christians were mistaken about their view towards the Crucifixion, that would not be their fault, but they would have been misled by a deceiving God.

Regarding the Qu'ranic view of Jesus and His Crucifixion, Crone concludes:

> "All in all, the Qu'ranic Christ is not the Son of God, nor is he the Messiah or the Logos in anything but name; he is not baptized, crucified, or resurrected, and he has no redemptive role: some verbal residues notwithstanding, all the central doctrines of mainstream Christianity are missing. One takes it that whatever they may have been, the local

---
[271] Cumming, Ibid., 27-28.
[272] Neely, Ibid., 5.

Christians were not of the mainstream kind."[273]

The rest of this study is concerned with the Crucifixion and how the Substitution Theory found its way into the Qu'ran.

Between Gnostic Thought and Islamic Theology

As previously discussed, the Substitution Theory was first attributed to Basilides, as Rasimus suggests. This story is referred to in a Nag Hammadi text, *Sec. Seth*, which found its way into later Islamic exegesis; according to the Qu'ran, Jesus only *seemed* to have died—later interpreters could present one of the disciples having substituted Jesus on the cross.[274] What supports this suggestion is that there is no theological basis upon which this theory is built in Islam. In Gnosticism, the dualistic worldview is the foundational doctrine of Docetism. The

---

[273] Crone, Ibid.
[274] De Conick, Ibid., 65.

spiritual nature of Jesus, in the dualistic worldview, cannot entail physical incarnation and death. However, in Islam, this dualistic view is not present, so what prevents Jesus from dying as a mere prophet like many other prophets previously killed by the Jews, especially that the Qu'ran depicted the Jews as killers of the prophets in many places: "that is because they disbelieved in the verses of Allah and killed the prophets without right."[275] There is no confirmed answer regarding this question, which is why Keith Prosser affirms that,

> "the argument within the Qu'ran that Jesus was not crucified, relies entirely on the Qu'ran's own affirmation that it is correct. This assertion is without historical verification, second party confirmation, or logical explanation."[276]

---

[275] Qu'ran 3:112. See also Qu'ran 3:181 and 4:155.
[276] Prosser, Ibid.

The Parallels

Although they do not share common theological ground, many scholars found striking similarities between the Qu'ranic stories and those of Gnostic Christianity. The Docetic view of the Crucifixion is but one example, and there are many others. These stories have been changed to some degree to suit the culture of seventh-century Arabia.

To begin with, let us examine the story of the Annunciation of Angel Gabriel to Mary revealing the birth of Jesus. In the Qu'ranic account, the Angel Gabriel declared a sign about Jesus, that cannot be found in any of the canonical four gospels: "He will speak to the people in the cradle and in maturity and will be of the righteous."[277] This what takes place later in the Chapter of Mariam [*Surat Al-Nisaa'*] in the Qu'ran, when the Jews accused Mary of immorality as she

---

[277] Qu'ran 3:45-46 Sahih International.

brought an illegitimate child. She replied to this accusation by pointing to the child:

> "So, she pointed to him. They said, 'How can we speak to one who is in the cradle a child?' [Jesus] said, 'Indeed, I am the servant of Allah. He has given me the Scripture and made me a prophet.' "[278]

A similar account is found in the apocryphal *Arabic Infancy Gospel of the Savior*:

> "Jesus spoke, and, indeed, when He was lying in His cradle said to Mary His mother: 'I am Jesus, the Son of God, the Logos, whom thou hast brought forth, as the Angel Gabriel announced to thee; and my Father has sent me for the salvation of the world.'"[279]

The parallels are clear; in both accounts, Jesus speaks while an infant in the cradle, He briefly introduces Himself, revealing His identity and His mission. The manipulation in the Qu'ranic story is also clear—and necessary—to fit its

---

[278] Qu'ran 19:29, 30 Youssef Ali.
[279] "The Arabic Infancy Gospel," chap. 1, accessed June 15, 2020, http://gnosis.org/library/infarab.htm.

theology for in the Qu'ran the Divine Sonship of Christ is everywhere denied.[280] So the "Son of God" became "the servant of Allah" and Christ's soteriological mission became a mere prophetic mission.

The Qu'ranic Annunciation to Mary states: "Behold! the angels said: 'O Mary! Allah giveth thee glad tidings of a Word from Him: his name will be Christ Jesus, the son of Mary.' "[281] Here, the angels declared Jesus as a Word from God, whereas in the Annunciation according to the canonical Scriptures, He was not labeled as such. Such a designation in the Annunciation narratives is present in the apocryphal *Gospel of James*:

> "Behold an angel of the Lord stood before her saying: Fear not, Mary, for thou hast found grace before the Lord of all things, and thou shalt conceive of His Word."[282]

---

[280] W.S.C. Tisdall, *The Original Sources of the Qur'ân* (Society for Promoting Christian Knowledge, 1905), 170, https://books.google.com.eg/books?id=vHowAQAAMAAJ.
[281] Qu'ran 3:45 Youssef Ali.
[282] "The Book of James--Protevangelium," chap. XL, accessed June 26, 2020, http://gnosis.org/library/gosjames.htm.

In the Qu'ran, Mary gave birth to Jesus beside a palm tree where a miracle of sorts occurred:

> "The pains of childbirth drove her to the trunk of a palm tree. She said, 'Oh, I wish I had died before this and was in oblivion, forgotten.' But he called her from below her, 'Do not grieve; your Lord has provided beneath you a stream. And shake toward you the trunk of the palm tree; it will drop upon you ripe, fresh dates. So, eat and drink and be contented.' "[283]

In this account, Mary was in an extremely painful situation due to the labor pains to the extent that she wished she was dead, but the Lord comforted her by providing dates and water. Crone finds this story a bit odd as,

> "Mary is driven to the palm tree by labor pains [*al-makhāḍ*], but the divine consolation takes the form of food and drink, not exactly what a woman needs in that situation."[284]

---

[283] Qu'ran 19:23-26 Sahih International.
[284] Crone, Ibid., 16.

However, another version of this miracle can be found in the apocryphal *Gospel of Pseudo-Matthew* with a slight variation:

> "while they were walking, that the blessed Mary was fatigued by the excessive heat of the sun in the desert; and seeing a palm tree, she said to Joseph: Let me rest a little under the shade of this tree. Joseph therefore made haste, and led her to the palm, and made her come down from her beast. And as the blessed Mary was sitting there, she looked up to the foliage of the palm, and saw it full of fruit, and said to Joseph: I wish it were possible to get some of the fruit of this palm. And Joseph said to her: I wonder that you say this, when you see how high the palm tree is; and that you think of eating of its fruit. I am thinking more of the want of water, because the skins are now empty, and we have none wherewith to refresh ourselves and our cattle. Then the child Jesus, with a joyful countenance, reposing in the bosom of His mother, said to the palm: O tree, bend your branches, and refresh my mother with your fruit. And immediately at these

words the palm bent its top down to the very feet of the blessed Mary; and they gathered from it fruit, with which they were all refreshed."[285]

In the apocryphal account, this miracle took place during the flight to Egypt, after the birth of Jesus, when the Holy Family was tired and in need of rest and refreshment. Jesus miraculously ordered the palm tree to bend down and refresh His mother with its fruit. The absence of this story from any canonical gospel suggests that the apocryphal story found its way into the Qu'ran with slight modifications in the details, and in a context that makes less sense than that of the apocryphal version.

Among the miracles of Jesus mentioned in the Qu'ran is the creation of birds from clay, as Allah tells Jesus:

> "You designed from clay [what was] like the form of a bird with My permission, then you breathed into

---

[285] "The Gospel of Pseudo-Matthew," chap. 20, accessed June 26, 2020, https://www.newadvent.org/fathers/0848.htm.

it, and it became a bird with My permission."[286]

Creating birds does not seem to be of any real benefit to suffering people, it is more likely to be a games of sorts as depicted in a parallel account found in the *Arabic Infancy Gospel*:

> "Now, when the Lord Jesus had completed seven years from His birth, on a certain day He was occupied with boys of His own age. For they were playing among clay, from which they were making images of asses, oxen, birds, and other animals [...] and He (Jesus) had made figures of birds and sparrows, which flew when He told them to fly, and stood still when He told them to stand."[287]

The apocryphal version of the miracle builds a richer context, providing more details and allowing a fuller illustration, while these details are absent from the Qu'ranic account. Another divergence is that in the Qu'ranic

---

[286] Qu'ran 5:110 Sahih International.
[287] "The Arabic Infancy Gospel," chap. 36.

version, the birds became alive by the breath of Jesus into them, whereas in the apocryphal account, they come to life by His word.

One of the prominent identities of Jesus in the Qu'ran is "God's Word and a Spirit proceeding from Him."[288] "His Word" is easily identified in the canonical gospels, but His identity as "Spirit proceeding from Him" is not a familiar concept in Orthodox theology,[289] given the existence of the Holy Spirit whom Jesus, in the canonical gospels, describes as "the Spirit of truth, who proceeds from the Father."[290] These two identities do not belong to the same person in Orthodox theology, whereas they are combined to phrase Jesus' identity in Islamic theology. This is foreign for orthodox Christianity but common in early Gnostic thought as discussed earlier: Cerinthus, one of the earliest Gnostics, described Christ as

---

[288] Qu'ran 4: 171 Youssef Ali.
[289] John 1:1
[290] John 15: 26

"the Logos (Word) or Spirit of God" as one identity.

These parallels, along with the inconsistent contexts of their Qu'ranic versions, strongly suggest that Islam heavily borrowed from early Gnostic ideas and apocryphal stories, altering details to fit its culture and merged them to produce stories with irrelevant details like the case of the birth of Jesus beside the palm tree, meaningless miracles like the case of birds' creation from clay, and stories without basis like the case of the Docetic view of the Crucifixion. However, the question is how could these stories in general and the Docetic doctrine of the Crucifixion specifically reach Arabia and influence Islamic views? The following section will investigate the thought and ideologies of seventh century AD Arabia, as well as trace the trajectory of early Gnostic ideas, specifically the Substitution Theory, and its survival despite all the resistance it faced.

Docetism in Arabia

By the second century AD, Gnosticism reached its peak and consequently, Docetic views became a widespread stream of thought. Basilides, who was active in Alexandria, became one of the most influential characters who adopted Docetism and invented a new interpretation of the Crucifixion, the Substitution Theory. His thought gained popularity and were composed in *Sec. Seth*. The Orthodox party fought this thought during the second and third centuries. However, it neither ceased to exist nor gain more followers as well. In the fourth century, Basilidians were still active in Egypt. Epiphanius of Salamis encountered them when he visited Egypt in AD 335 and it seems that they tried to convert him.[291] Their ideas continued for couple more centuries as some scholars argue:

> "that various Christian sects holding unorthodox Christological views were active in the Arabian Peninsula during Muhammad's day

---

[291] Kelhoffer, Ibid., 127.

and likely influenced him, including Monophysites, Julianists, Gnostic Basilideans, Nestorians, and other groups."[292]

Annemarie Schimmel acknowledges this opinion:

> "The influence of Christianity was quite strong, for the areas adjacent to the peninsula (Syria, Mesopotamia, and Egypt) were largely inhabited by Christians of various confessional loyalties so that the Arabs came to know, more or less intimately, Monophysites, Nestorians, and other Christian sectarians."[293]

While dealing with the historical presence of Christian thought in Arabia, we must keep in mind that apocryphal accounts were essentially transmitted orally. Reuven Firestone comments on the oral traditions in Arabia:

> "The fluid nature of oral literature therefore lends itself to adaptation to its naturally changing cultural environment [...] one could predict

---
[292] Lanier, Ibid.
[293] Schimmel, Ibid.

the Biblicist legends transplanted into Arabian clime would naturally bend and evolve into new forms as they were told and retold under the influence of new geographic and cultural surroundings."[294]

It is natural that the apocryphal stories adapt themselves to take new forms while being transmitted into a new culture like that of Arabia as shown earlier. One important means of transmitting these oral traditions was the trade routes throughout Arabia which facilitated the spread of religious ideas. Muriel Debie states that:

> "Syriac Christianity spread along the maritime and terrestrial trade roads from the Mediterranean all the way to South India (purportedly converted by Saint Thomas), and to Central Asia, Tibet, China, and Mongolia."[295]

---

[294] Jonathan M. Reck, "The Annunciation to Mary: A Christian Echo in the Qur'ān," *Vigiliae Christianae* 68, no. 4 (2014): 372.

[295] Muriel Debie, "For a Different History of the Seventh Century C.E.," *Institute for Advanced Study*, 2017, https://www.ias.edu/ideas/2017/debie-syriac.

Some Arabian tribes were converted to Christianity before Islam. Syriac was their liturgical and religious language; it was spoken all the way from Syria to Southern Arabia.[296]

In addition to the trade routes that caused many unorthodox ideas to spread, Arabia was a refuge for not a few heretics of different sects.[297] Arabia as a refuge for heretics explains the presence of Islamic ideas that belonged to earlier heretical groups. Debie mentions an important letter that was sent by Philoxenus of Mabbug (AD 440-523), the Syriac bishop and theologian, to a *stratelates* of al-Ḥīra.[298] The letter spoke of a certain heretical group called Julianists or *Aphthartodocetae* among the Miaphysites who understood the unity of the divine and human natures in Christ in a way that made them

---

[296] Ibid., para. 5.
[297] Tisdall, *The Original Sources of the Qur'ân*, 140.
[298] Debie, Ibid. Mabbug is Hierapolis in ancient Syria, Stratelates is a Byzantine title for an official leader in one of the "capital" camps/cities of the Arabs in pre-Islamic late antiquity, al-Ḥīra today is in Iraq.

question Jesus' suffering on the cross.²⁹⁹ The Julianists are named after their leader, Julian of Halicarnassus, an anti-Chalcedonian theologian of the sixth century.³⁰⁰ He believed that the body of Christ was incorruptible [*aphthartos*], so He was incapable of committing sins and was not subject to pain and death which promotes a Docetic understanding of the suffering of Christ and implies that He only seemed to suffer and die on the cross.³⁰¹ Debie recounts:

> "in the 520s, a large group of Julianists took refuge against Byzantine persecutions in al-Ḥīra and in Upper Egypt. Some subsequently fled to Ethiopia and on to Arabia. These groups had an enduring presence until at least the eighth century in Southern Arabia where many churches belonged to them."³⁰²

---

²⁹⁹ Ibid.
³⁰⁰ Crone, Ibid., 252.
³⁰¹ Ibid.
³⁰² Ibid.

However, Crone does not think that the Docetism in the Qu'ran related to the Julianists as she argues:

> "Julianist Docetism was not of the right kind: no Julianist denied that Christ had been crucified, only that he had suffered in the process, or that he had suffered as a human subject to the laws of nature rather than by choice, an issue in which the Qu'ran displays no interest. So, the Julianists cannot account for the Qur'anic position."[303]

For the Julianists, it is a matter of whether Christ suffered by nature or by choice; He might not be subject to suffering, yet He chose to suffer. This theology is different than that presented in the Qu'ran, yet their understanding of the nature of Christ may have had indirect influence on the Crucifixion story in Islam.

Crone presents another common source of the Docetic ideas in Arabia, the Manichaeans, who were by the sixth century the only well-known

---

[303] Crone, Ibid., 8.

Docetae left.[304] Manichaeans seemed to embrace the Host Theory of Docetism rather than the Substitution Theory, which supposed Christ to be a heavenly being, united Himself with the man Jesus at baptism and was separated from him before the Crucifixion.[305] Although the suggestion that Islam meant to adopt this kind of Docetism—the Host Theory instead of the Substitution Theory—can still be valid, yet, as contended earlier, the majority of the Islamic commentaries endorse the Substitution Theory. Additionally, the earliest commentaries on the Qu'ran confirm the presence of Docetic Christians adopting the Substitution Theory in Arabia. Al-Tabari, in his commentary on the denial verse, mentions two stories of the Crucifixion from Docetic Christians who lived in Arabia. The first story belonged to a Christian who converted to Islam as narrated by Ibn-Ishak.[306] He reported that one of Christ's

---

[304] Ibid., 7.
[305] Ibid.
[306] Muhammad ibn Isḥāq ibn Yasār ibn Khiyār was an Arab Muslim historian and hagiographer in the eighth century.

disciples called Sergius accepted to take the form and likeness of Christ, and to becrucified in His stead in order to accompany Him in paradise.[307] This Christian was no doubt a Docetic Christian, rather than Orthodox. Al-Tabari states that some Christians claimed that Judas Iscariot is the one who was made to resemble Jesus, so they crucified him intead [*ba'ad Al-Nasara yazo'm an Yodos Zakareyayota hwa allazi shubbeh lahom fasaloboh*].[308] These Christians were among the Arab Docetae as well.

Moreover, Muhammad used to listen to stories from people around him, some of them were unorthodox like the Docetic Christians mentioned by Al-Tabari, as Ignaz Goldziher recounts:

Ibn Ishaq collected oral traditions that formed the basis of an important biography of the prophet Muhammad.

[307] Tafsir Al-Tabari, "Altafsir.Com - The Tafsirs," v. Q 4:157, accessed June 26, 2020,
https://www.altafsir.com/Tafasir.asp?tMadhNo=1&tTafsirNo=1&tSoraNo=4&tAyahNo=157&tDisplay=yes&Page=4&Size=1&LanguageId=1.
[308] Ibid.

"Just as the Christian elements of the Qu'ran reached Mohammed largely through the apocryphal traditions and heresies disseminated throughout oriental Christendom, similarly many of the elements of oriental Gnosticism found an entrance into Islamism. Mohammed appropriated a medley of ideas that reached him through his casual contact with men during his mercantile travels and utilized most of this material in a very unsystematic manner." [309]

We read in the commentary of the Qu'ranic verse by Al-Wahidi what confirms the opinion of Goldziher:[310]

"Abd Allah ibn Muslim who said: 'We owned two Christian youths

---

[309] Ignaz Goldziher, *Mohammed and Islam*, trans. Kate Seelye (Yale University Press, 1917), 13, 14, https://babel.hathitrust.org/cgi/pt?id=uiug.30112004055817&view=1up&seq=9&size=150. Ignaz Goldziher was a Hungarian scholar of Islam. He is considered one of the founders of modern Islamic scholarship.

[310] Qu'ran 16:103. Ali ibn Ahmad al-Wahidi, who lived in the eleventh century, is the earliest scholar of the branch of the Qu'ranic sciences known as Asbāb al-Nuzūl (i.e. the contexts and occasions of the Revelation of the Qu'ran). Al-Wāhidī aimed to collect and systemize information concerning all the known reasons and contexts for the Revelation of particular Qu'ranic verses.

> from the people of Ayn Tamr, one called Yasar and the other Jabr. Their trade was making swords, but they also could read the Scriptures in their own tongue. The Messenger of Allah, Allah bless him and give him peace, used to pass by them and listen to their reading."[311]

This made the idolaters always say about Muhammad that "he is being taught by them!"[312] According to this commentary, Muhammad used to listen to the Scriptures. It is not clear what exactly "the Scriptures" refer to: could possibly be canonical or apocryphal, Christian or Jewish. Muhammad used to listen to religious stories to the extent that his enemies accused him of attaining knowledge from them and not from heavenly revelations.

Ian Mevorach presents the viewpoints of two scholars, Hans Küng and Kenneth Cragg, who

---

[311] Al-Wahidi, "Asbab Al-Nuzul, Altafsir.Com - The Tafsirs," Q 16:103. accessed June 26, 2020,
https://www.altafsir.com/Tafasir.asp?tMadhNo=1&tTafsirNo=86&tSoraNo=16&tAyahNo=103&tDisplay=yes&UserProfile=0&LanguageId=2.
[312] Ibid.

appreciated and respected Islam, summarizing their opinions as follows:

> "Küng asserts that Muhammad was likely influenced by the writings of Basilides, a Christian Gnostic who taught that Simon of Cyrene was crucified instead of Jesus; therefore, he argues, the classical exegetes of the Qur'an may have been correct in their interpretation, though mistaken historically. Kenneth Cragg also endorses the idea that Qu'ran 4:157-58 may derive from 'docetic tendencies in early heretical Christianity which, for mainly metaphysical reasons, questioned the possibility of the Messiah being literally and actually a sufferer.' Küng and Cragg deeply appreciate and respect Islam, yet they find no better interpretation of these verses than John of Damascus—that is, Muhammad—was influenced by heretical Christian ideas."[313]

---

[313] Ian Mevorach, "Qur'an, Crucifixion, and Talmud A New Reading of Q 4:157-58," *Journal of Religion & Society* 19 (2017): 10, 11.

From the previous discussion, it is clear that Gnostic and Docetic ideas were present in Arabia during Muhammad's lifetime. Gnostic thought either came through trading or through refugees. Moreover, Muhammad used to listen to religious stories from traders; so much so that his enemies accused him of learning from them. This suggests that Muhammad borrowed Docetic understanding of the Crucifixion from the surrounding Docetae in his community. Scholars agree that Muhammad was influenced by the Docetic stories in his milieu, especially that of Basilides. At this point, we may ask why did Muhammad specifically adopt the Substitution Theory of Basilides instead of the Orthodox view?

Substitution Theory in Islam

Unlike Gnosticism, the Docetic view in the Qu'ran is without a theological foundation. In this regard, Crone asks why then did Muhammad opt for Docetism instead of simply accepting that

Jesus died by crucifixion?[314] The choice of Docetism is so odd as it inclines to Gnostic groups like Marcionites, Manichaeans, and others whom later Muslims were to denounce as heretics [*zindīqs*]; and that "the doctrine also looks superfluous, for it has no bearing on any other religious issue discussed in the Qu'ran."[315] As this opens the door for speculation, we will delve into four proposed reasons why Muhammad adopted the Docetic view over the Orthodox one.

One idea proposed by Masud is that Muhammad wanted to protect the higher status of Jesus as a prophet "when he found his own enemies, the Jews, exulting at having slain Jesus."[316] Muhammad simply adopted a popular Gnostic belief from his milieu which denies the crucifixion of Christ, although his views had little

---

[314] Crone, Ibid., 6.
[315] Ibid.
[316] Masud Masihiyyen, "Immature Resurrection of Gnosticism in Islam." sec. 3.

in common with the general thought of Gnosticism.[317]

Goldziher thinks that it is a matter of personal preferences and self-convictions of Muhammad. He proposed that,

> "the proclamation of the Arabian Prophet is an eclectic composition of religious views to which he was aroused through his contact with Jewish, Christian and other elements, by which he himself was strongly moved and which he regarded as suitable for the awakening of an earnest religious disposition among his people."[318]

The third probability is that it may be only a reflection of what was already happening in seventh-century Arabia as Debie recounts that the,

> "obscure passage of *Surat al-Nisaa'* 4, 157 about Jesus's crucifixion suggests that it was a matter of controversy and that nobody was sure about what happened then [...] the discussions of these very

---
[317] Ibid.
[318] Goldziher, *Mohammed and Islam*, 3.

subjects between the dissident and mainstream Miaphysites in Arabia before Islam can explain the basis on which the Qu'ran expressed its own puzzlement about what exactly happened on the cross."[319]

The fourth suggestion is that Muhammad may have thought that this view is the correct Orthodox view because the surrounding milieu may have this Docetic opinion as the dominant one as Lanier states that:

"Muhammad and his followers may have believed that such an apparitional crucifixion was, in fact, 'perfectly in line with the early and apparently widespread Christian perspective' they had encountered. In other words, Muhammad thought his teaching on the crucifixion was the Christian teaching as well—unaware that it was a version of 'Christianity' deemed heretical."[320]

---

[319] Debie, Ibid.
[320] Lanier, ""It Was Made to Appear Like That to Them," sec. 3.

These four suggestions illustrate the Substitution Theory's existence in the Qu'ran and its ossification as a belief for Muslims since the seventh century. It is also important to present the gap between Gnostic Docetism and Islamic Docetism in terms of theological basis. The original Gnostic motive for this theory is the belief in Christ divinity and a dualistic worldview which makes it impossible for Him to assume a materialistic evil body that is subject to suffering and death, whereas these beliefs are contrary to the idea that

> "considers Jesus an ordinary prophet that was miraculously saved from death in the hands of his adversaries [...] Gnosticism tended to endorse Jesus' divinity, whose human body was only an illusion, in sharp contrast to Islam, which tried to portray Jesus as one of the only-human prophets of the past."[321]

---

[321] Masud Masihiyyen, "Immature Resurrection of Gnosticism in Islam." sec. 2.

Conclusion

The Crucifixion of Christ is a pivotal and central event for Christianity; Islam denies it, claiming that someone else took Jesus' form and was crucified in His stead. The evidence presented in this work proves that such an Islamic claim does not reflect the real historic event but rather borrows from a second century Docetic interpretation of the Crucifixion from Basilidian Gnosticism.

After thorough exploration of the sources with respect to the historicity of the Crucifixion of

Christ, it is an indisputable historical fact that earns broad scholarly consensus, and it forms a major fixed point in ancient history. The origin of the theory was invented by the school of Basilides of Alexandria, either himself or his followers, based on Gnostic principles. These principles can be summarized as follows: first, there exists a chasm between the spiritual realm where the gods live, and the physical world created by one of the emanated gods. Secondly, Christ is a God who belongs to the spiritual realm. Therefore, He cannot connect with the physical world, but He can just seem as someone physical with whatever shape He wants. Since there is someone who actually suffered and truly died on the cross under the name of Jesus Christ, Basilides explains this incident as Jesus exchanged His likeness with Simon of Cyrene letting him be crucified in His stead.

I have presented the major ancient texts that contain the Docetic dogma, such as *Sec. Seth*, *The Apocalypse of Peter*, *The Gospel of Judas*, as well as shed some light on the Gospel of Barnabas and showed that this dogma is attached with the hostility of the Creator of the material world and the rejection of the Old Testament prophets as worshippers of that Creator. This hostility shows the chasm between the material and the spiritual worlds, which consequently made it impossible that Christ would have a real physical body and with it, the ability to be crucified. In Orthodox Christianity, as Clement teaches, the body is a blessed creation of the ultimate God, not bad by nature, and considered worthy receptable for the Holy Spirit. The hostility is only against the wrongdoings and the deviated desires of the body, and not the body itself; the incarnation is not only acceptable in Orthodox Christianity but a central tenant of faith.

The arguments supporting the Substitution Theory are found throughout this work in the discussion of Gnosticism. The Islamic discussion remains unclear, as there is no theological foundation that supports such a theory in Islam. The counterarguments also can be found following the presented arguments, but they are condensed in the section of "The Orthodox Response to the Theory." The main arguments can be summarized as follows: Basilides claimed that he received his teachings from the Petrine tradition through Glaukias, an interpreter of Peter. However, it is unlikely for Peter, who belonged to Jewish culture, to teach the principles of Gnosticism such as the Demiurge creator, the cosmos duality, the hostility to matter, or the existence of many gods emanated from the ultimate God. Besides, Peter taught about the death of Jesus in his sermon in the book of Acts. Some scholars think that the Docetic interpretation is based on a literal interpretation of Mark 15, but just before this passage in Mark, Jesus spoke of His burial and poured blood which can never indicate an intent to escape the Crucifixion nor His Docetic appearance. The biblical tradition testifies for the reality of Jesus' body as John, the disciple of Christ, provided direct sensible evidence from an eyewitness in his epistle when he spoke of the physical interaction with Christ. The disciples of the apostles such as Ignatius and Polycarp and their successors refute the Docetic claims by holding onto the Scriptures that were handed down by the apostles in which the reality of the Incarnation and the Crucifixion are central as well as proven. The Gnostic claim of receiving esoteric beliefs secretly from the apostles was refuted by Irenaeus, who thinks that such a claim would means that the apostles were hypocrites, teaching the blind according to blindness and the enlightened according enlightenment, rather than teaching truth. Hippolytus refutes Gnostic thought simply by tracing the historical trajectory of their doctrines, proving their heretical origins. Additionally, some Muslim scholars find the Substitution Theory to be problematic. Al-Ghazali argues that if it was true then we cannot always trust our senses in everyday life as we may think someone is real although it was his likeness. Mahmoud Ayoub affirms that it unintentionally accuses God of deceiving the Christians all these centuries.

I demonstrated a historical link between Islam and Gnosticism. First, there are many Gnostic elements and apocryphal stories in the Qu'ran which suggest the spreading of unorthodox ideas in Arabia at the birth of Islam. Second, I historically traced the Substitution Theory from the second century AD, its inception, to the seventh century AD, and demonstrated that it might have reached Arabia through trading or through those who sought refuge in Arabia. The earliest Islamic commentary, Al-Tabari, acknowledges that Docetic Christians were present in Arabia and that some of them converted to Islam. Moreover, it was common for Muhammad, the prophet of Islam, to sit with traders and listen to their religious stories and ideas.

Based on these findings, it is evident that Islam borrowed the Substitution Theory described in Qu'ran 4: 157, 158 from the second century AD Docetic interpretation of Basilides that was already present in Arabia during the seventh century AD.

This study can contribute to academic dialogue on many levels; it provides historical and theological materials that could be used in the field of comparative religion. It also could be beneficial for Christian-Muslim dialogue, especially in such a debatable matter, the Crucifixion of Christ. Moreover, it promotes critical thinking for Muslims about their long-held beliefs such as the Substitution Theory of the Crucifixion.

This study opens doors for further research. There is a need for digging deeper into the earliest Islamic stories and *hadith* to gain better insight about the religious ideas and sects that existed at the dawn of Islam, which would in turn provide a better understanding of the Qu'ranic context, the motives of its verses, and the origins of its doctrines. This means that there is a necessity for translating more Arabic texts into English to provide richer material for studying.

Bibliography

Al-Wahidi. "Asbab Al-Nuzul, Altafsir.Com - The Tafsirs." Accessed June 26, 2020. https://www.altafsir.com/Tafasir.asp?tMadhNo=1&tTafsirNo=86&tSoraNo=16&tAyahNo=103&tDisplay=yes&UserProfile=0&LanguageId=2.

"Amora | Jewish Scholar." *Encyclopedia Britannica*. Accessed September 12, 2020. https://www.britannica.com/topic/amora.

Angus, Samuel. *The Religious Quests of the Graeco-Roman World: A Study in the Historical Background of Early Christianity*. New York: Biblo and Tannen, 1967.

Bauer, Walter, Robert A Kraft, and Gerhard Krodel. *Orthodoxy and Heresy in Earliest Christianity*. Mifflintown, PA: Sigler Press, 1996.

Bos, Abraham P. "Basilides as an Aristotelianizing Gnostic." *Vigiliae Christianae* 54, no. 1 (2000): 44–60.

Broek, R. Van Den. "The Present State of Gnostic Studies." *Vigiliae Christianae* 37, no. 1 (1983): 41–71.

Brown, S. Kent, and C. Wilfred Griggs. "The Apocalypse of Peter: Introduction and Translation." *Brigham Young University Studies* 15, no. 2 (1975): 131–145.

"Colloquia: The International Conference on Gnosticism at Yale: A Report." *The Biblical Archaeologist* 42, no. 4 (1979): 253–255.

Crone, Patricia. "Jewish Christianity and The Qur'an (Part Two)." *Journal of Near Eastern Studies* 75 (2016): 1–21. doi:10.1086/684957.

———. "Jewish Christianity and the Qur'ān (Part One)." *Journal of Near Eastern Studies* 74, no. 2 (2015): 225–253.

De Conick, April D. *Religion: Secret Religion*, 2016. http://link.galegroup.com/apps/pub/8NWM/GVRL?sid=gale_marc&u=crepuq_mcgill.

"Docetism | Religion | Britannica." Accessed July 1, 2020. https://www.britannica.com/topic/Docetism.

Downey, Glanville. *A History of Antioch in Syria: From Seleucus to the Arab Conquest.* xvii, 752 p. Princeton, N.J.: Princeton University Press, 1961. //catalog.hathitrust.org/Record/001241909.

Drijvers, Han J. W. "Early Syriac Christianity: Some Recent Publications." *Vigiliae Christianae* 50, no. 2 (1996): 159–177.

Endress, Gerhard, and Carole Hillenbrand. *Islam: An Historical Introduction*. New Delhi: New Age Books, 2006.

Eric D. Huntsman. ""The Lamb of God: Unique Aspects of the Passion Narrative in John," in Behold the Lamb of God: An Easter Celebration." Accessed October 18, 2020. https://rsc.byu.edu/behold-lamb-god/lamb-god-unique-aspects-passion-narrative-john#_edn41.

Fiensy, David. "Lex Talionis in the 'Apocalypse of Peter.'" *The Harvard Theological Review* 76, no. 2 (1983): 255–258.

Flavius Josephus. *The Complete Works of Josephus.* Trans. William Whiston. Grand Rapids: Kregel Publications, 1981.

Fr. Tadros Y. Malaty. *A Panoramic View Of Patristics In The First Six Centuries*. Preparatory edition. St. George's Coptic Orthodox Church, Sporting, Alexandria, 2005.

Frankfurter, David. "An Historian's View of the 'Gospel of Judas.'" *Near Eastern Archaeology* 70, no. 3 (2007): 174–177.

Gibbon, Edward, and J. B. Bury. *The History of the Decline and Fall of the Roman Empire*. Vol. 2. 7 v. London : New York: Methuen & Co.; G.H. Doran Co., 1901. //catalog.hathitrust.org/Record/009793910.

Goldziher, Ignaz. *Mohammed and Islam*. Translated by Kate Seelye. Yale University Press, 1917. https://babel.hathitrust.org/cgi/pt?id=uiug.30112004055817&view=1up&seq=9&size=150.

Grant, Robert M. "Gnostic Origins and the Basilidians of Irenaeus." *Vigiliae Christianae* 13, no. 2 (1959): 121–125.

Gregory R. Lanier. "'It Was Made to Appear Like That to Them:' Islam's Denial of Jesus' Crucifixion." *Reformed Faith & Practice*. Accessed April 25, 2020. https://journal.rts.edu/article/it-was-made-to-appear-like-that-to-them-islams-denial-of-jesus-crucifixion-in-the-quran-and-dogmatic-tradition/.

Havelaar, Henriette W. *The Coptic Apocalypse of Peter: Nag-Hammadi-Codex VII,3*, 2012. https://doi.org/10.1515/9783110884449.

Ian Mevorach. "Qur'an, Crucifixion, and Talmud A New Reading of Q 4:157-58." *Journal of Religion & Society* 19 (2017).

"Ibn Kathīr | Muslim Scholar | Britannica." Accessed June 26, 2020.

https://www.britannica.com/biography/Ibn-Kathir.

Ignatius of Antioch. The Epistle of Ignatius to the Smyrnaeans. *Ante-Nicene Fathers: The Writings of the Fathers Down to A.D. 325, Vol. 1.*Eds. Coxe, A.C., Donaldson, J, and Roberts, A. Grand Rapids: Eerdmans Publishing, 1989.

Ignatius of Antioch. The Epistle of Ignatius to the Trallians. *Ante-Nicene Fathers: The Writings of the Fathers Down to A.D. 325, Vol. 1.*Eds. Coxe, A.C., Donaldson, J, and Roberts, A. Grand Rapids: Eerdmans Publishing, 1989.

Irenaeus of Lyons. *Against Heresies. Ante-Nicene Fathers: The Writings of the Fathers Down to A.D. 325, Vol. 1.*Eds. Coxe, A.C., Donaldson, J, and Roberts, A. Grand Rapids: Eerdmans Publishing, 1989.

Joseph L. Cumming. "Did Jesus Die on the Cross? The History of Reflection on the End of His Earthly Life in Sunni Tafsir Literature," 2001.

Kelhoffer, James A. "Basilides's Gospel and 'Exegetica (Treatises).'" *Vigiliae Christianae* 59, no. 2 (2005): 115–134.

Layton, Bentley. "The Significance of Basilides in Ancient Christian Thought." *Representations*, no. 28 (1989): 135–151.

Mansel, Henry Longueville. *The Gnostic Heresies of the First and Second Centuries. With a Sketch of His Work, Life and Character by the Earl of Carnarvon.* Edited by J. B Lightfoot. London, 1875.

Marjanen, Antti, and Petri Luomanen. *A Companion to Second-Century Christian "Heretics."* Leiden; Boston: Brill, 2008. http://site.ebrary.com/id/10363801.

Masud Masihiyyen. "Immature Resurrection of Gnosticism in Islam." Accessed May 11, 2020. https://www.answering-islam.org/authors/masihiyyen/gnostic_islamic_crucifixion.html.

Mawdudi, Sayyid Abul A'la. *Towards Understanding Islam*. The Islamic Foundation, 2013. http://site.ebrary.com/id/10983812.

Mubārakfūrī, Ṣafī al-Raḥmān, and Ismā'īl ibn 'Umar Ibn Kathīr. *Tafsir ibn Kathir: (abridged)*. Riyadh: Darussalam, 2000.

Muriel Debie. "For a Different History of the Seventh Century C.E." *Institute for Advanced Study*, 2017. https://www.ias.edu/ideas/2017/debie-syriac.

N. T. Wright. *The New Testament and the People of God*, 2013.

Neander, Augustus, and Henry John Rose. *The History of the Christian Religion and Church during the First Three Centuries*. London: St. Paul's Church-yard, 1841.

Neely, Brent. "At Cross Purposes: Islam and the Crucifixion of Christ, a Theological Response." *Transformation Transformation: An International Journal of Holistic Mission Studies* 34, no. 3 (2017): 176–213.

Polycarp of Smyrna. The Epistle to the Philippians. *Ante-Nicene Fathers: The Writings of the Fathers Down to A.D. 325, Vol. 1*.Eds. Coxe, A.C., Donaldson, J, and Roberts, A. Grand Rapids: Eerdmans Publishing, 1989.

Prosser, K. *Was Jesus Crucified?* Lulu.com, 2016. https://books.google.com.eg/books?id=KsGyDAAAQBAJ.

Reck, Jonathan M. "The Annunciation to Mary: A Christian Echo in the Qur'ān." *Vigiliae Christianae* 68, no. 4 (2014): 355–383.

Roger A. Bullard, and Joseph A. Gibbons, trans. "The Second Treatise of the Great Seth - The Nag Hammadi Library." Accessed June 3, 2020. http://gnosis.org/naghamm/2seth.html.

Schimmel, A. *And Muhammad Is His Messenger: The Veneration of the Prophet in Islamic Piety*. Studies in Religion. University of North Carolina Press, 2014. https://books.google.com.eg/books?id=gZojDQAAQBAJ.

Justin Martyr. The First Apology. *Ante-Nicene Fathers: The Writings of the Fathers Down to A.D. 325, Vol. 1*.Eds. Coxe, A.C., Donaldson, J, and Roberts, A. Grand Rapids: Eerdmans Publishing, 1989.

Strathearn, Gaye. "The Gnostic Context of the Gospel of Judas." *Brigham Young University Studies* 45, no. 2 (2006): 26–34.

Tafsir Al-Tabari. "Altafsir.Com - The Tafsirs." Accessed June 26, 2020. https://www.altafsir.com/Tafasir.asp?tMadhNo=1&tTafsirNo=1&tSoraNo=4&tAyahNo=157&tDisplay=yes&Page=4&Size=1&LanguageId=1.

Tafsir Al-Tobrosi. "Altafsir.Com - The Tafsirs," n.d. https://www.altafsir.com/Tafasir.asp?tMadhNo=0&tTafsirNo=3&tSoraNo=4&tAyahNo=171&tDisplay=yes&UserProfile=0&LanguageId=1.

"Tanna | Judaic Scholar." *Encyclopedia Britannica*. Accessed September 11, 2020. https://www.britannica.com/topic/tanna-Judaic-scholar.

"The Arabic Infancy Gospel." Accessed June 15, 2020. http://gnosis.org/library/infarab.htm.

"The Book of James--Protevangelium." Accessed June 26, 2020. http://gnosis.org/library/gosjames.htm.

The Gospel of Pseudo-Matthew. Accessed June 26, 2020. https://www.newadvent.org/fathers/0848.htm.

Tisdall, W.S.C. *The Original Sources of the Qur'ân*. Society for Promoting Christian Knowledge, 1905. https://books.google.com.eg/books?id=vHowAQAAMAAJ.

Van Voorst, Robert E. *Jesus Outside the New Testament: An Introduction to the Ancient Evidence*. Grand Rapids [etc.: Eerdmans, 2000.

Vladimir Lossky. *Orthodox Theology: An Introduction*. Crestwood, NY: St. Vladimir's Seminary Press, 2002.

———. *The Mystical Theology of the Eastern Church*. London: J Clarke, 2005.

Walker, Williston, Cyril Charles Richardson, Wilhelm Pauck, and Robert T Handy. *A History of the Christian Church*. New York: Charles Scribner's Sons, 1959.

Whittingham, Martin. "How Could So Many Christians Be Wrong? The Role of Tawātur (Recurrent Transmission of Reports) in Understanding Muslim Views of the Crucifixion." *Islam and Christian-Muslim Relations* 19, no. 2 (2008): 167–78.

Williams, Frank. "The Gospel of Judas: Its Polemic, Its Exegesis, and Its Place in Church History." *Vigiliae Christianae* 62, no. 4 (2008): 371–403.

Wilson, R. McL. "Gnostic Origins Again." *Vigiliae Christianae* 11, no. 2 (1957): 93–110.
Wisse, Frederik. "The Nag Hammadi Library and the Heresiologists." *Vigiliae Christianae* 25, no. 3 (1971): 205–223.
Wynne, George Robert. "The Christology of the Petrine Speeches." *The Irish Church Quarterly* 4, no. 16 (1911): 296–305.
Yamauchi, Edwin M. *Pre-Christian Gnosticism: A Survey of the Proposed Evidences.* Eugene, Or.: Wipf and Stock, 2003.
Zahniser, A. H. Mathias. *The Mission and Death of Jesus in Islam and Christianity.* Eugene: Wipf and Stock Publishers, 2017.

For any corrections, suggestions or feedback, please contact me at:

e.r.khalil@hotmail.com

www.ingramcontent.com/pod-product-compliance
Lightning Source LLC
Chambersburg PA
CBHW030523080526
44586CB00011B/304